The Forgotten Youth
OF A NATION

John Youhanes Magok

A Note from the Publisher

The publisher wishes to acknowledge and thank Dr Douglas H. Johnson for his invaluable help and support for Africa World Books and its mission of preserving and promoting African cultural and literary traditions and history. Dr Johnson and fellow historians have been instrumental in ensuring that African people remain connected to their past and their identity. Africa World Books is proud to carry on this mission.

© John Youhanes Magok, 2020

ISBN: 978-0-6489291-2-3

All rights reserved. No part of this publication may be reproduced, stored in a retrieval system, or transmitted, in any form, or by any means, electronic, mechanical, photocopying, recording or otherwise, without the prior permission of the publishers.
This book is sold subject to the conditions that it shall not, by way of trade or otherwise, be lent, re-sold, hired out or otherwise circulated without the publisher's prior consent in any form of binding or cover other than in which it is published and without a similar condition including the condition being imposed on the subsequent purchaser.

Editor: Eric Junior Wagobe
Design and typesetting: Africa World Books

Dedication

I dedicate this noble book to the strong and vibrant millennials, colleagues, and friends by whom the future of our country is crafted by virtue of their resilience and hard work. To all those who endured the troubled times during which civil wars raged on as you never lost the hope of building a mighty nation. To my parents, Mr. Youhanes Magok Nhial the golden supportive Daddy and a lifelong entrepreneur, and Madam Rebecca Riel Gatluak, the mother and nurture of our prodigious family.

Foreword

In a country where a tiny minority of the youth are educated, here comes an intellectual product by a young and upcoming South Sudanese intellectual. This book not only shares personal experiences and observations on the author's native country, but also offers delightful insights into what could take the war-torn nation out of its messy present.

The book walks the reader through a maze of social, political, cultural and moral vices that have gripped the nation, especially after conflict broke out and has raged on for nearly seven years, punctuated only by short periods of implementation of cessation of hostilities agreements brokered by regional peace mediators.

Coming under captivating chapter headings, some of the narrative in the book may cause wet eyelids, as one can see with hindsight a nation in vicious self-destruction and young people without a future! The inverted image of some neo-elite among high-ranking military officials, politically appointed post-holders and top civil servants basking in opulence, while majority of the people wallow in abject poverty, living in squalid displacement settlements, vast refugee camps, peri-urban sack and plastic huts, are nerve-wrecking!

Yet, despite a period of peace implementation signed by the major warring parties, the situation remains unchanged! The author, himself a refugee from his early childhood days, shares the plight of his peers in both refugee camps and urban centers, which may touch the reader with melancholia!

His tell-all revelations include in-depth personal observations of how hopelessness combined with desperation have driven some of the South Sudanese youth to become easy prey to warlord assembled militias, making them to indulge in outrageous criminal activities, such as gang robberies, looting, pillage, rape and murder.

Peppering this grim image is the opportunistic neo-elite; the hard-hearted, the callous and corrupt so-called *"national leaders"* whom the author gives the euphemism *"inflated bellies"*. The majority of those in the league of unpitying leaders are from none other than the '*Oyee* party' – the ruling Sudan People's Liberation Movement (SPLM).

The book speaks of how these self-baptized 'liberators' have taken their lofty government positions as opportunities to enrich themselves, or what in their wayward mindset, is a way to compensate for their years in the 21-year war period against Arab Sudanese-led governments.

In a strategy to intimidate and silence any critic, the crooks invoke their favorite phrases *"we have liberated this country"* and *"It is our time to eat"*. And, to justify their occupation of senior positions without academic qualifications, they gloat another self-defeating and pathetic mantra: *"This country will not be liberated by certificates"*!

Obviously, this mentality has injected a sense of impunity and disdain in those occupying political and senior managerial offices. To completely silence any detractor, the old-fashioned self-seeking leaders take to tribalism which the book has gone full length to describe. Intolerance of opposing views and dealing harshly with contrary opinions, is a common thing. The book attributes the tragedy of the South Sudanese youth to this class of irresponsible military and political leaders.

FOREWORD

Nevertheless, the book also comes handy with personal pieces of advice and sheds some beam of hope to the author's peers – the youth. It laments the exploitation of the nation's diversity by shrewd political wannabes and warlords. But it also makes a case for this diversity to be regarded as a virtue and source of strength. The author appeals to his fellow young people to realize their potential. I find this to be the novel value of the book. This is a mark of potential leadership in the author.

Laila B. Lokosang, PhD.

(Author of *"South Sudan: The Case for Independence and Learning from Mistakes"*).

Preface

The book is a guide for the thick-bellied *Uncles* in red ties and the incumbent politicians, who are young at heart but also willing to cooperate with millennials. Writing this book was conceived as an idea that I gained from my exposure to the various youth empowerment programs across the African continent including the *African Union Youth Volunteer Corps, African Presidential Leadership Program, Tana High-Level Forum on African Security and Governance, Young African Leadership Initiative of Eastern Africa*, among others.

Like many other young South Sudanese, I grew up in a challenging environment with limited space for personal growth, professional development, and civic engagement. The book sheds light on the common rituals of South Sudanese youth from different perspectives regarding their social lifestyles, education, politics, employment, media literacy, and conflict. It presents facts about the world's newest country, South Sudan, which I joyfully describe as the land of great abundance and the Eden of diversity while shedding more light on the unrecognized contributions of its youth, and how its poor leadership has contributed to the country's anarchy.

Due to the never-ending conflicts, villages were abandoned by folks who fled to United Nations Camps while others fled as refugees to foreign lands. As South Sudan grapples with widespread fear and grief, the book provokes compelling thoughts to rethink and reshape our future, the responsibility of which rests with us alone to put it on a better guiding path. Whether through agony or joy, we are obliged to spearhead the nation's building by demilitarizing the mindsets while shifting the narratives on odd rituals.

Mass education and civic engagement by the media literacy can help a lot in promoting unity and social cohesion to espouse the *Ubuntu* spirit of 'I am because we are'. I believe that investing in and working with the South Sudanese youths will guarantee the inclusion and active involvement at all society levels, economically and politically. Lastly, the book calls for an urgent commitment by stakeholders to improve the economy, ensure unimpeded access to education, employment opportunities, respect of human rights, support for youth-owned businesses, health care, and social reconciliation, to counter inter-community violence. As a peace-loving South Sudanese, I hope you find this book rewarding in your quest for a just South Sudan.

Introduction

I doubt if the current leaders of the new South Sudan were once young like the majority of South Sudan's population - the youths! These leaders have deliberately undermined the role of youth in nation-building, sidelining their potential and willingness to participate in our country's decision and policymaking. We call their leadership *"the rule of the liberation heroes"* - made up of the elite class whose sole aim is to compensate themselves for their noble task in liberating the country. In so doing, they are plundering and squandering every single penny generated from the young nation's resources.

While governments in other countries are seriously empowering their young populations to be the next trailblazers in science and technology, in South Sudan they are left to hawk goods on city streets and fighting the old folks' tribal and political wars. This book highlights how South Sudan is being ruled on the selfish political and military interests of its corrupt leaders who are adamant about sharing the national cake with anyone who does not share their religious, tribal, and geographical sentiments.

The aim is to encourage the government to consider the youths as the nation's key building blocks without which its very future cannot be guaranteed. It would be so regrettable that young people's energy, intelligence, and passion are laid to waste at a time when they are most needed. Let's all not forget the phrase *"When life gives you lemons, make lemonade"* which encourages optimism and a positive attitude in the midst of adversity or misfortune. You will read about the trials and tribulations of the South Sudanese youth in the new nation, a reality that stimulates actions to achieve a better and sustainable South Sudan that accommodates everyone regardless. The book further calls for the demilitarization of our mindsets to encourage a return to civilian rule and the acknowledgment of human rights as essential to co-existence. Readers will become aware of the challenges and opportunities in achieving a united South Sudan that prioritizes the inputs of the young people in generational co-leadership that triumph endless reconciliations and healings by thinking in a global spectrum coined with the diverse local actions that position the youth and women at the heart of national affairs.

The book further encourages policies, vision, and programs that positively impact the marginalized folks in rural areas, slums, and informal settlements. Having spent most of my life witnessing wars like almost every other young South Sudanese, the experience of being born and raised in a war zone is so surreal that it haunts you for the rest of your life. It is an experience that keeps the author awake every night, and hence the need to address the causes of wars and conflicts in a guiding book for the young people with proven potential to transform our beloved nation.

This book presents the current paradigm and suppression of the millennials by the liberation dinosaurs who have failed to prioritize the agendas that advance the youth empowerment and transformation for the nation's benefit. The book carries a loud call to unified actions coupled with the *Ubuntu* spirit in leaving no one behind.

Table of Contents

Adversities of A New Nation	1
A Passionate Appeal to Youths	13
'Inflated' Bellies	24
Social Vices and Rituals	35
Demilitarizing Our Mindsets	43
Entrenched 'Gabilia'	54
Stylish But 'Uneducated'	58
Silencing the Guns	65
Deceitful Political Dreams	76
Lethal Propaganda Tools	83
Gender Mainstreaming	89
Boosting Youth Productivity	101
Exclusion from Governance	110
Leadership Without Vision	113
Humble Beginnings	122
Perfecting the Storm	128
Ubuntu and Reconciliation	135
Think Globally, Act Locally	145
The Way Forward	151

Adversities of A New Nation

... on the trials that afflict our motherland

South Sudan is the world's youngest nation that is landlocked and located in the East-Central region of Africa. It is an ethnically diverse country with a population of more than 12 million people. The country gained her independence from Sudan on *July 09, 2011*, after the signing of the *Comprehensive Peace Agreement (CPA)* that ended the *Second Sudanese Civil War* - Africa's longest-running civil conflict. South Sudan covers a land area of *619,745 km²* and as a tropical country, it is rich in biodiversity, blessed with favorable weather, distinct ethnicities, and spectacular fauna, thus crowning it the *Land of Great Abundance and Eden of Diversity*. It boasts of an unparalleled ecosystem that hosts various unique animal species, in addition to the densely forested jungles where creatures that are nowhere else to be found hide. Its climate is relatively warm, with seasonal precipitation in the southern regions and less rain in the north *(Greater Upper Nile* and *Greater Bahr el Ghazal)*.

South Sudan is truly gifted by nature due to its well-stocked natural resources including rivers, lakes, fertile agricultural land, and minerals. The world-famous *White Nile* flows through the country in the *South-North* direction and forms a vast swamp called *Sudd* which is a massive solid floating vegetation island. The diversity of her well-endowed natural resources is incomparable to anywhere else in Africa. Due to its financial prowess, South Sudan was once referred to as *The London of East Africa* owing to its relatively strong currency whose exchange rate with the US Dollar topped at *SSP2.7 = $1* before the *2013 South Sudanese Civil War*. Then, the influx of traders to Juba city was at its highest with a flourishing economy that earned the country substantial fortunes with promising successes for national prosperity. It remains a well-known fact that even today, foreigners control almost all the country's economic transactions through their remotely managed banks dotted at every corner of the country.

Nevertheless, many of South Sudan's natural resources are yet to fully be exploited thus offering enormous potential for unprecedented economic growth. The country's *Gross Domestic Product (GDP)* is largely tied to oil exportation which accounts for 98% of all total revenues. Nonetheless, the oil sector has failed to boost the country's other vital sectors, as oil is exported for refining abroad, allowing Somali traders to import fuel into an already oil-producing South Sudan. Thus, there seem to be no strict laws to regulate and protect the country's vulnerable economic sector in the event of an emergency crisis. One example was the unexpected strike by Ethiopian water tank drivers in Juba in 2013, which disrupted the city's normal water supply, leaving the government with no choice but to bow to their pressure and negotiate with them to restore order.

There is no doubt that foreigners have for a long time controlled almost everything that the South Sudanese use in their daily lives. While the *Ethiopians* control the hotel and tourism sectors, the *Somalis* have taken over the fuel market and the importation of construction materials, while the *Ugandans* also provide us with all food and other consumer goods. Not forgetting the *Kenyans* who control the banking/financial sector, the *Bangladeshis* and *Indians* who provide networking and communication/internet services, and the *Eritreans* who still have their lion's share in electricity supply. There appears also the *Chinese* who are developing our physical infrastructure and oil production, while our *Sudanese* brothers *(especially the Darfourins)* are occupying the importation of electronics and other retail undertakings. Simply put, we eat, dress, drive, and live in a country where foreigners are the means to our survival as they provide the much-needed supplies for our comfort and improvement.

The people of this *new nation* are madly in love with the *ready meal* - that is, the flowing oil - a sector that almost everyone dreams of working in, owing to the lavish lifestyles of those already working there. Such an unsustainable trend must be clipped by developing other important economic sectors, which not only contribute to the diversification of our economy, but also allow us to manage our sectors including agriculture, mining, production, and tourism. The *new nation* is one of the most ethnically diverse in Africa, home to 64 different ethnic groups with different *Nilo-Saharan* languages that are widely spoken, a rich mix of distinctive traditional cultures and spiritual affiliations. The country's colorful flag also bears deep-rooted meanings - black for the people, red for the bloodshed during the struggle for independence, green for the agricultural sector and the natural vegetation, white for peace earned through years of liberation struggles, blue for the waters of the Nile River and the yellow star which stands for hope, unity, and determination of the South Sudanese. The flag was adapted from the *Sudan People's Liberation Movement/Army (SPLM/A)*, the founding party. Though this created a brief confusion between the state and party after the hard-won freedom in the *Promised Land*.

The biggest puzzle lies in trying to understand the difference between the nation of South Sudan and the political party *SPLM/A*. It is difficult to say whether the *SPLM/A* is South Sudan and vice versa, but logically South Sudan belongs to all people from each of the 64 ethnic groups, and the *SPLM/A* is but a political entity that has fought resolutely throughout the independence struggles. Accordingly, it is important to set boundaries between political parties and the state since not every South Sudanese ascribes to a certain political party, but all South Sudanese ascribe to one state of South Sudan. All parties have equal opportunities to become the governing party through fair and free elections, and only through democratic processes will the South Sudanese enjoy the fruits of belonging to one state - South Sudan. Its president must reflect the people's choice, the members of parliament should be drawn from each of the country's constituencies, and the government must maintain the three fully-functional branches that espouse the citizens' freedom of expression.

Should the people of South Sudan decide to seriously abdicate the issues of political identity, then either the spirit of nationalism should be left to the political elite, or the people will need to find a new way of divorcing politics from the state. We cannot underestimate the need for involving people from all the four corners of South Sudan represented by their legislative assembly members, the council of states, and participation of special interest groups including women, youths, the private sector, and religious leaders. A resolution like this can dismantle the impression that the *SPLM/A* owns South Sudan and give its political elites the upper hand in abusing state resources by squandering every cent in the state coffers. In *July 2011*, I was among the excited people waving the flag of independence as we marched to the *Freedom Square* in Juba to celebrate with the tens of thousands of others who were thrilled at the prospect of a new life and a new beginning in the new nation of South Sudan. Only three years later, the joy for the hard-won self-governance was cut short by the *Oyee*[1] Party's shortfalls which ignited a fire within their internal affairs in 2013 and escalated to devastate the whole country. These actions forced half of the population to seek refuge in the *United Nations Protection of Civilians'* (*POCs*) sites while others had to flee to refugee camps in the different neighboring countries for safety.

Until then, I had learned that peace is not simply a choice, but a prerequisite for our very existence in this world. The absence of it breeds unspeakable tragedies and dismay. As such, every South Sudanese should embrace peace, beginning with oneself and then externally triggering it in love, laughter, and harmony. Living in South Sudan may never be an *American Dream* to some people's standards due to a myriad of unresolved differences that still keep haunting us. During the struggle for a new nation, I repeatedly heard the distressing sounds of gunshots being recklessly fired followed by the dreadful screams of desperate people fleeing their burnt down villages and running away into the unknown; an experience that I do not wish for anyone. Now, in my youthfulness, a similar scenario is playing out, and it is even much worse considering that the young people are the most enticed into this endless culture of violence and revenge. No one seems worried about the mindless loss of life, and the collapse of the economy - a terrible reality that we live in today.

---

[1] Oyee is a political term that is used to motivate crowds.

But, one saying goes like: "*Every country undergoes a mess before deciding on sustainable development.*" South Sudan is no exception because the task of building a nation from scratch comes at a high price and can profoundly affect subsequent generations. The South Sudanese youth remain the country's only hope for reigniting a new era of reconciliation, healing, peace, co-existence, and sustainable development. Due to their tender age, young people are full of enthusiasm, determination, and knowledge and have a wealth of untapped opportunities and potential. All they deserve is being heard and heeded by someone who cares deeply about their well-being while engaging them in the reconstruction and rehabilitation of the nation. There has never been an appropriate time as this to renew our vows as South Sudanese, to protect and develop our beloved nation.

On *July 9, 2020*, South Sudan celebrated its ninth anniversary as an independent country and considering that the young nation has been involved in deadly civil wars for the better part of the last decade. However, a new power-sharing agreement was formalized at the beginning of 2020 under the renewed agreement on conflict resolution. Could this have been the nation's long-awaited turning point? The civil war and the ongoing conflicts have plunged the South Sudanese people further into abject poverty. It has become even worse for those who are already struggling to meet their basic needs, including shelter, water, health care, and food.

Millions of people have been forced to leave their homes after watching them burning down and their belongings, including livestock and crops, plundered or destroyed. Many have fled to neighboring countries including *Uganda, Sudan, Ethiopia, D.R. Congo,* and *Kenya* where they live as refugees. Others have traveled as far as *Libya*, desperately trying to reach Europe in search of greener pastures. Imagine how exhausting the journey must be, trudging through scorching deserts and riding through the rugged Mediterranean Sea, not forgetting the rude welcome that awaits them upon arrival in Europe. A few brave people have risked seeking refuge within South Sudan, but other catastrophes, including the devastating floods, continue to take their toll on their livelihoods, with insufficient crops, pushing up food prices, leading to increased hunger in complicated times like these. Such scenarios have produced frightening realities that repeatedly traumatize vulnerable young people to the point where they exhale anger and rage.

As young leaders of this new and promising nation, let us not lose our hope but look ahead and together break the eternal cycle of violence and persistent poverty. The 2020 formation of the *Revitalized Transitional Government of National Unity (R-TGoNU)* was a positive step towards an inclusive and diverse arrangement, but the South Sudanese still crave a fully-functional government that supports the meaningful participation of the vulnerable women and youth in governance structures. Recently, South Sudan was ranked lowest in terms of the human development index and termed as a *'fragile state'* – a coined designation by development agencies and some international bodies, including the United Nations. Other statistics are damning: South Sudan has the highest maternal mortality rate in the world, and the illiteracy rate among the female population is estimated at 90%. But more than half the population must feed, dress, and shelter on less than a dollar a day, and worry every time about potential outbreaks of conflict. The critical problems of widespread poverty, insecurity, and inadequate infrastructure cannot be solved by a dysfunctional and inefficient government that has operated with institutions still in the making for the last nine years. Though the *Revitalized Transitional Government of National Unity (R-TGoNU)* is still holding on – it is likely to be faced with the sheer scale challenges of poor infrastructure in a deplorable state, the increased spate of violence through communal conflicts, and the rising humanitarians' crises.

Corruption has already undermined the President's *Crude Oil for Roads in South Sudan* project, with an example of the newly constructed *Juba-Rumbek* road being washed away by heavy rains. This incident unmasked the negligence of contracted road construction companies who failed to deliver the expected performance. Corruption aside, South Sudan has vast oil reserves, extensive arable land, and the flowing water through its center, all of which offer enormous potential for national growth and prosperity. To be a self-sustaining nation, South Sudan must turn around and provide security, food, and employment for its desperate population which can only happen if we the South Sudanese reflect and nurture patriotic ideologies for collective national development. This will only happen if we begin to prepare the younger, promising generations to rise to the challenges and bring about the necessary development and lasting peace. The nation must find its strength in diversity and build institutions that represent the spectrum of its vast geographical and ethnic wealth. One of the foundations of nation-building is to guarantee freedom of speech, full political rights, and popular institutions that provide competent services to all, regardless of political, religious, or cultural affiliation. This must happen in a new and revitalized nation of South Sudan.

The Dependency Syndrome

If you take time and go through the previous treaties and agreements, you will never find a single accord attributed to local efforts or something like *'South Sudanese Solutions for South Sudan's Problems'*. It was always the international community and the regional blocs that came to our aid because none of us seemed to be concerned about our situation. Why do we not seem to have the same human empathy as our international friends? Is this not our own country? All the statements by our top officials down to the local chiefs include carbon copies to *Inter-Governmental Authority on Development (IGAD), TROIKA,* and *United Nations Mission in South Sudan (UNMISS)*. Most *Junubin (South Sudanese)* are naive in that they are unable to discern the difference between a local problem and a regional concern, but we must be careful that these organizations are not concerned with our woeful plight. It doesn't matter even if armed men take your cattle or land. Most of them laugh at us through the back door because we are unable to judge what is right from what is wrong.

Away from the diplomatic spotlight, we South Sudanese must adopt effective strategies for managing our affairs, because the external friends we entrust to solve our problems do not have our best interests at heart, and the protracted war by the various *SPLM/A* factions is a case in this point. If not for empathy, then the international organizations in South Sudan could be playing their smart cards, including the exclusion of South Sudanese from being employed in their offices. Their representatives have become so powerful that they continue feeding on the sustained applause by our government officials, who are themselves unmatched professional beggars - a job that keeps them fat albeit the risks.

Independence is defined as being free from any external influence and is characterized by autonomy, self-determination, self-government, and sovereignty. For decades,

South Sudanese, like their African compatriots, have fought for freedom across the continent since the 1950s. Our struggle started on *August 18, 1955*, with the *Torit mutiny* against the then colonial government in Sudan, and then with the *Anya-Nya I* and two other movements that signed the *1972 Addis Ababa Peace Agreement*. However, many South Sudanese perceived the agreement as being inequitable in the face of the widespread segregation policy pursued by the Khartoum regime. Most eyewitnesses of that time still testify that there was a policy of Arabization, Islamization, and continued abuse of power by the government in the North. This violated the provisions of the peace agreement that had held the country together for many years.

Despite *Anya-Nya II*'s continued opposition to the established system throughout the agreement, peace and tranquility flourished. On *16 May 1983*, Battalion 105 mutinied in *Bor*, and a broad mobilization of rebellions ensued throughout Sudan. The *SPLM/A* was believed to have emerged at an opportune time when Sudan's marginalized majority could no longer contain the extent of deep-rooted exploitation by the North's regime. The struggle also depicted the highest level of leadership within the ranks of the *SPLM/A* which inspired the oppressed and disgruntled masses to risk all they had and fight for what they believed were their rights. This is the reason why I pay tribute and my respects to *Dr. John Garang De Mabior* for his wise leadership and to all the martyrs, veterans, and other *SPLM/A* freedom fighters who shed their blood without regret so that we achieve the greatest basic freedom and rights within our nation.

The prolonged *Second Sudanese Civil War* ended with the signing of the historic *Comprehensive Peace Agreement (CPA)* on *9 January 2005* between the *SPLM/A* and the *Government of Sudan*. The peace agreement allowed for a secession referendum, in which the South Sudanese had to choose between self-determination and remaining part of contiguous Sudan. The reality was manifested when the South Sudanese overwhelmingly voted for separation with 98.83% of the votes cast in an internationally supervised free and fair referendum. This victory paved the way for the later establishment of the *Republic of South Sudan* on *9 July 2011*. The *SPLM/A* assumed leadership responsibilities for the new nation with the promise of implementing all that they fought for during the half-century of the independence struggle. Even today, expectations among the population are high, given the approaches that have shaped the current government. Alternatively, the pathological addiction syndrome has absorbed our nation from the outset, which is why I urge readers to do something to save our young nation from the fetters and abysses of addiction syndrome because we need to take full control and responsibility for our affairs.

Local dependence is the latest form touted by the political elite, spurred on by the current leadership, which protects the political executive and shields it from public accountability. Fearing being challenged, the political elite then concentrates the country's resources and production factors under its tight grip, so that those who need them must make some sacrifices. The supreme leadership also consciously refuses to empower people who are not their own, possibly for fear that an empowered population may be too conscious of being easily manipulated. To understand this better, one should focus on how some leadership positions have been assumed in the country, even those whose relatives have influence dating back to the days of the 1972 *Addis Ababa Agreement* continue and manipulate the system in their favor. The opposition groups which once claimed to be seeking political reform are themselves a living example, as they too are desperate for their turn, wasting public resources. The current leadership has neglected the youth of this nation because they believe these young people could become their future nemesis. But such ill-intentioned motives will only set us back, and competition is not only among us alone, but everywhere, regionally, globally, and as such we must build up competent minds for it, now or never.

Regional dependence, comparatively, has proved to be an endemic situation, bringing South Sudan to its knees and clinging to the mercy of its neighbors and the region for survival, and as such, they easily manipulate our sovereignty by exerting their influence over us. For instance, we are regarded as a *Consumer member* to the *East African Community* and other regional blocs since they supply us with most of what we consume. Yet they buy almost nothing from us with claims that we have nothing of value to offer. Others say we are too *inferior* to regulate regional affairs, and thus offering to do so on our behalf. We only become regionally relevant when we pay membership fees to the organization *(X)* after repeated name-calling and public humiliation. To turn the tables, the current *R-TGoNU* should reinvent our economy by building oil refineries within the country so that we sell our fuel products to the region because such an initiative can become a catalyst for a much-needed symbiotic relationship between South Sudan and its neighbors. South Sudan's economic capabilities can also make it a powerhouse with a greater say in regional or continental affairs. Any form of dependence on foreign aid for our survival and regional dependence is disastrous, as it becomes an obstacle to full independence and, concurrently, harms our hard-won sovereignty.

Natural Resources as a Blessing and a Curse

South Sudan has enormous natural resources and an ecosystem that makes it a biodiversified prosperous nation. These wealth resources represent the natural capital out of which other forms of capital are driven and acquired. This could make a significant contribution to improving our tax revenues, incomes, and poverty reduction. Unfortunately, many resource-rich countries have failed to meet their citizens' expectations, while others have managed to prosper from these resources. South Sudan is one of the unfortunate countries where its natural resources, including oil, have contributed to the destruction of the state system. Countries like *Japan* without natural resources have been able to develop with the help of their well-managed human resource. *Japan* was reduced to almost nothing after the devastating *Second World War*, as vital infrastructure was destroyed and it became difficult to administer without adequate natural resources. They had to start from scratch by investing heavily in education to provide practical skills and improve the ability of the population to work hard for their country. If you visit Japan today, you will hardly recognize the Japan of the late 1930s, as a remarkable transformation has engrossed the entire nation.

A study by *The Atlantic* shows that among the many frustrations of development, perhaps none is greater than the *resource curse*. The *Human Development Index (HDI)* is measured based on the extent of poverty and inequality levels, which are often a feature of countries with enormously endowed natural resources, including *Nigeria* and *South Sudan*. Rather than contributing to basic services, broadly shared growth, and social cohesion, rich oil, and mineral resources have often brought misery and insecurity to these nations. True, South Sudan was for a while divided within itself after independence, but this has come at the expense of infrastructure damage and social breakdown across the country

I believe if the parties to the revived peace agreement have a love of the land at heart, then they would prepare the ground for peace dividends in the transitional phase. Undoubtedly, if the appropriate procedures are followed and the interests of the people are given priority, it will not be long before a respected South Sudan is rebuilt and put in its rightful place among the renowned nations. What the people of South Sudan need are better roads, unimpeded access to health services and education, clean drinking water, and security. Otherwise, without these priorities, South Sudan's resources will forever remain a curse and an obstacle to its progress. South Sudan's natural resources can easily become a source of insecurity if they are not used constructively and shared equally for the common well-being of its citizens.

Land Is a Golden Resource

Land conflicts often have negative effects on the economic, social, spatial, and environmental development of the country, especially in developing and transition countries. South Sudan is, therefore, no exception, where land management institutions are weak, opportunities for economic gain through illegal measures are widespread and poor people have no access to land. Here, many conflicts are perceived as tribal clashes between ethnic groups over communal land and the associated natural resources. Distress and greed can equally breed land conflicts, but the scarcity and increase in the value of land can worsen the situation. Land conflicts occur especially when there is a chance to obtain land for free, regardless of whether this land belongs to the state, the community, or as private property.

Here, I will highlight some land-related issues that plague the *Equatoria* region. Land conflicts have raged on in this part of South Sudan with her neighbors including *Uganda, Kenya, D.R. Congo,* and *Ethiopia,* then among the states, between the counties, Payam to Payam, Boma to Boma, and among individuals. Worse of all, land grabbing is so common among those with impunity as they misuse their authority to grab land belonging to the poor and defenseless. This also happens regularly between communities including pastoralists and nomads, as powerful communities create geographical lines unrelated to their claims to ancestral land. In post-conflict situations or the early stages of economic transition, when regulatory institutions, controls, and sanction mechanisms did not yet exist, powerful people seized land when their positions allowed it, or when the occupants were in a weak and vulnerable position to safeguard it.

In countries where land is slowly becoming materially valuable and increasingly becoming private property *(including what is happening everywhere in South Sudan)*, people are also trying to accumulate as much land as possible. Having mentioned all this, anyone who is concerned may have to ask themselves the following questions:

★ What do you think are the most sustainable solutions to the internal disputes of the new nation?
★ Do we have strong laws to end persistent land disputes?
★ Why is our leadership ignoring these trivial issues that threaten the nation?

For example, millions of internally displaced people have been forcefully and involuntarily resettled due to the endless civil wars. I fear that those in the IDP camps may have no place, as it remains unclear whether those who took over their land and occupied it will willingly surrender it or they will be compelled by law to vacate it.

A Passionate Appeal to Youths

...in nation-building, everyone plays a role

The youths of South Sudan are among the youngest in Africa, accounting for at least 72% of the country's total population, with an average age of *18-25*. This young population remains the most vulnerable and most affected by rampant ineffective governance, which continues to flourish unabated through unemployment and civil violence. Young people in this new nation have long been exploited for selfish gain by those in leadership positions who have been deaf to their cries for help. Although young, energetic, and innovative, South Sudan's youth remain under-represented in the country's leadership. Sometimes, as young people, we have to blame ourselves for waiting for others to decide what is good for us and use us like puppets or springboards. However, now is the appropriate time for the young people of this country to occupy a prominent place at the high table of the country's decision-making.

On 22nd February 2020 *(the eve of the formation of the R-TGoNU)*, I had a candid conversation with an Ethiopian friend who lectures at *Addis Ababa University*. We were talking about the peace that was to return to South Sudan after *Dr. Riek Machar* and *President Salva Kiir* promised to bring stability to the country through the formation of a revitalized transitional government. Nearby, *Al Jazeera* was streaming the President live with a bold caption: *"Peace is finally here"*. Then I thought, *'At last, multitudes of starving and displaced South Sudanese were about to enjoy some peace again'*, but for how long? I wasn't sure, and no one else was!

Going back to our conversation, I remembered how the race for the lucrative ministerial posts intensified in Juba, as belly-baring politicians were busy rocking their suits and red ties while seeking nominations and appointments at the State House in Juba. Here is how the conversation went:

Friend: Mr. Youhanes, congratulations upon the return of peace to South Sudan!

Me: Thank you, my friend, this is indeed good news for the whole region.

Friend: Indeed. South Sudan was the perfect destination for business before the conflict in 2013, and many of my friends made a lot of money back then. I hope that can happen again.

Me: Sure, South Sudan used to be the main hub of trade and business – the 'London of Eastern Africa' because its currency was strong, especially against the US Dollar.

Friend: Wow! Concrete facts! Why doesn't the new government appoint young and promising people like Youhanes to ministerial positions? You're brilliant!

Me: Hahaha, my friend, in South Sudan, anyone between 18 – 35 years is considered a child. I am now 28 years old, and the incumbent 'Uncles' can only consider me as being fit for a driver or bodyguard. This despite being qualified for more significant roles with my B.Sc. and M.Sc. in Engineering through which I can have an upper hand in serving my country.

Friend: How come? Then, who are the youngsters? (He seemed to ask almost all the "why" questions when I interrupted him with loud laughter!).

Me: My friend, the South Sudanese youths are regarded as those within the age range of your Prime Minister (Dr. Abiy Ahamed Ali), and in fact, many who are beyond 45 still consider themselves to be youths. Some pretend to represent us in the government, but they never portray the rightful image of the youths' plight.

Friend: What are the criteria for young people to enter politics in South Sudan and how are ministers appointed?

Me: Well, as long as you're as old as a dinosaur (laughs), have a potbelly, three smartphones in your hand, and expensive clothes, you're perfectly suited to any ministerial post! Nevertheless, you need personal bodyguards to double your chances. We have little chance of being appointed, so all we have to do is lick the boots of our political bosses.

Friend: That's so outrageous! What about the academic qualifications and know-how? What's the point of having them if your leadership never acknowledges them?

Me: *I guess the era of technocratic and competent government is still far ahead because as long as the current leaders consider us as befitting for lower duties, including fighting on the front lines, bodyguards, drivers, and escorts in their private homes, we have no chance. Most of our people are illiterate, and often powerful figures assume authority because of their military power rather than their education and leadership competence. The only qualification required is to be a former combatant or being connected to a well-known politician who is pleased to appoint whoever he wishes to any government position, regardless of their qualifications to serve.*

Friend: *That is so absurd, but there are many other possibilities outside politics, including in the economy or the oil sector.*

Me: *Absolutely! There are other ways to achieve the desired change and contribute to the economic development of our country. However, young people cannot change their livelihoods without first correcting the political maladministration embedded in our administrative system.*

And that is how our conversation went. My friend is a keen follower of all events happening in South Sudan as he hopes for lasting peace, reconciliation, and nation-wide healing. Nevertheless, only inclusive participation of every South Sudanese youth is key towards achieving this and our leaders are aware but choose to defy this dire need. In its first chapter, *Revitalized Agreement on the Resolution of Conflict in South Sudan (R-ARCSS)* highlights that the youths are the major victims of the relentless civil conflicts and hence constitute a tremendous portion of refugees. The agreement also required the Minister for Youths and Sports in the *R-TGoNU* to be less than forty years, yet, a youth is commonly known as someone under the age of 35. Whereas the United Kingdom's under 17 youths are already enjoying their rights to participate in their country's democratic governance, in South Sudan, we are blatantly deprived of the same privilege.

As youths, we should never accept having *dinosaurs* in the cabinet deciding for us, and yet they are out of touch from the reality we experience regularly. My main concern is the unremitting trend of handpicking youths whose appointments are full of ill political motives which hinder their active participation in the nation's building. Such unproductive *'youthful'* ministers include the Minister for Petroleum, the Minister for

Youths and Sports, and the Minister for Higher Education, Science, and Technology. All they do is boasting about their supremacy while the common folks patronize them with swank titles including *'Zoal-Kabiir'*, *'Beny'*, and *'Kuar-Mi-Diit'* (meaning *boss/big man* in *Sudanese Arabic, Dinka,* and *Nuer languages* respectively). While they visibly appear young, their minds are interwoven with their bosses' mindsets that blind them from considering the youths as being essential for this country's development, progress, and the strengthening of its governance structures. They only care about regularly fattening their protruding bellies, living a posh lifestyle, including buying new houses, luxurious cars, and being called *the boss*. Apparently, to them, inclusivity and youth engagement are only but a taboo.

At first, it seemed like the parties and mediators presumed the youths to be only interested in music, sports, and entertainment. And as such, they excluded them from running the country's affairs. They only pretended to care about us by assigning the Ministry of Youths and Sports to a so-called *'youthful'* minister, but what about the other positions that affect us as youths? Noteworthy, the youths are the most valuable human capital resource this country has owing to their immense creativity that can accelerate us into sustainable development.

If you observe intently, there seems to be plenty of competent and disciplined youths well-capable of holding important ministerial dockets including finance, defense, interior, economy, and foreign affairs. The youths are not the outright perpetrators of violence or a 'time bomb' as falsely portrayed by our leaders, but almost all whom I know genuinely yearn to participate in peace-building to champion reconciliation and change the unfortunate course of history. Our mission should be in choosing competent youths who genuinely desire to improve the general lives of their fellow South Sudanese and propel the country to its eternal glory.

Elsewhere, youths have been the trailblazers in science, technology, economics, trade, and peace but in South Sudan, they are deliberately marginalized as they are not given the chance to flourish minus the *'old folks'* interests coming into play. The South Sudanese youths are facing abnormal levels of anxiety and depression due to the style of leadership that fails to meet their expectations. We must allow the youths to showcase their talents and skills which are indeed vital for taking the country ahead and avoid further wrecks. It is time to invest in these young people as they are teeming with intellectual masterclass ideas that can improve not only their livelihoods but even the betterment of every South Sudanese human being to usher in the kind of South Sudan we all yearn for.

Among the South Sudanese youths, some live large, far away from the life of conflicts and devastation. These are the children of the high-class citizens, the ruling elites from the *Oyee party (SPLM/A)*, and other senior military officers. This breed of youths is out of touch with the reality that their counterparts in conflict-ridden hot spots face. I compare any attempts at compelling them to understand the other side of life to teaching pigs how to sing, which is always a lose-lose proposition. In the developed world, the motivating phrase is: *"If you don't get a decent education, then you won't find a good job"*, as education is the measurement of success and good fortune in life. However, in my country, things are different as the motivating phrase is: *"If you don't get an 'Uncle' in the government, then you won't get a good job"*, as having Uncles in the government is the measurement of success and good fortune in life. I know many hardworking young professionals who deserve decent employment within the public and private sector but these have to bribe the pot-bellied *Uncles* in red ties.

Transparency and equality in the recruitment process remain an unresolved myth. Many have willingly allowed themselves to be aided by corruption and other dubious means to make it to the top, and once they get there, they behave like demigods, mistreating other struggling people without showing them kindness. Although this is an unfair trend, it has become the cycle of life in the new nation of South Sudan. Sometimes one is led to believe that he or she was born in the wrong country and is living there at the wrong time, as young people are rendered unworthy by some well-known opportunists, but I will hold my pen so I don't name and shame them.

Our elders gave us a wonderful and healing proverb that says: *"Judge each day not by the harvest, but by the seeds you have sown."* As the younger generation of this country, we must console ourselves that we have done our best with a clear motive - to unite all the people of South Sudan. We have done our best to sow the finest seeds, but the seedlings have often been trampled underfoot immediately after germination. The seeds we have sown have been met with excruciating moments of death, isolation, and silence in desperate situations without light, oxygen, and nothing else to encourage us to keep on fighting. Our well-intentioned works may go unrecognized or not be celebrated, but we should never surrender the battle for what is righteous and lawful.

The South Sudanese youth must free themselves from the troublesome yoke of the powerful uncles and rich fathers and learn how to fish for themselves. Such an attitude will encourage us to recognize how independent and autonomous we must be through the proper exploitation of our potentialities for sustainable development. Having a relative who can afford your needs is not bad, because it is part of our culture in South Sudan that families stick together in times of need and happiness. However, I urge young people to do something worthy for themselves instead of waiting for every penny from their parents, especially when they are young, energetic, and productive. Are you not ashamed to still live with your uncle, who feeds and houses you and thirty other people in the household? It's madness if you're not! This could put immense pressure on the head of the family to raise funds to support his large family.

We need brave Davids *(young people)* who are willing to risk it all and face the reality by asking their uncles or fathers to teach them how to fish for themselves. Today's young people must claim their right to earn a decent living and contribute to a better life for themselves and the country. This requires changing the entire context of the hearts, bodies, minds, and minds of these young people, to evoke a spirit of togetherness, to promote the social cohesion deeply rooted in the societies that tickle to the ground. Challenging as this life might be, it is the young leaders who are developing meaningful strategies to build a more sustainable country, and our forefathers have inherited the privilege of advising the youth by teaching them that they have the right to fish freely for their lives.

As future leaders of this nation, we must emulate the bravery of the liberation generation, the likes of *Anyanya*. The ongoing instability throughout the country has shattered the status quo and torn down the curtain on the notion that so many of the old people in charge of our country's affairs know what they are doing, but the truth is they don't know what it takes to build a progressive nation as all they have done is to sow seeds of hatred and endless hostility over the years. They exposed our country to serious problems stemming from the massive economic inequalities, tribalism, political favoritism, ongoing inter-ethnic conflicts, and ethnic wars, all of which led to the scarcity of basic needs including security, health, food, and education for ordinary citizens.

It is our time to wake up as young people to the fact that the traditional ways of doing things simply won't work in these modern times, it doesn't matter how much money you make yet you are surrounded by starving, sick, and homeless people. We need better and innovative ways of managing the affairs of the new nation if we think not only of ourselves but also of each other. Did all these old people know that they were in charge and knew what they were doing? It turns out they don't have the answers. Many of them don't even ask the right questions. The mishandling of the Coronavirus disease in 2020 is an attestation to the regime's ineptitude as many public officials became the main carriers of the disease and hence put many lives at stake.

To my surprise, the presidency, with neither justifications nor preparations, declared the easing of the prevention measures, with the reopening of bars and nightclubs at the top of the president's orders. So if we need a better South Sudan, it is up to us the young people to achieve it, and the perception may be intimidating, but this is the only way through which we can behold true light at the end of the dark tunnel of violence and war. We should not wait until we have reached the end of a tunnel, our actions can light it up where we are at the moment. With all the myriad challenges facing our country today, no one can tell you that you are too young to *understand* or *that's how it's always been*, the old school style.

No matter the old folks' misdeeds, this is the world that our generation must shape, and we have the initial dynamism and power that rests upon our hands. We will not give in to fear, because many countries in the world have previously gone through difficult times, including slavery, civil war, famine, disease, and the enormous economic meltdown. We must emerge stronger in times of uncertainty because the new generation has learned from the previous mistakes of our liberators and figured out how to do things better. Above all, do what you think is appropriate, and feel good about it with values that endure, including honest, hard work, integrity, responsibility, fairness, generosity, forgiveness, and respect for others and their beliefs. After all, we should be part of the solution, not the problem, while we also build a lasting legacy through community development. We can't put our trust in the leadership of our older folks who failed to manage the state's affairs, but I do envision one-man who will lead us to the Promised Land – just like Moses who crossed the red sea with the Israelites, holding a stick in the hand and the wisdom of God in his brain. The population, particularly youths, can play Moses' role and be the unifying stick. We must stop gobbling each other up like locusts in a glass, and if we do not, we are doomed to fail to achieve the desired sustainable development in South Sudan.

Youth Reconfiguration

Most countries in the world regard the youths to be an important segment within society that can be a force for propelling sustainable development and unifying the communities. They are the backbone that cannot simply be neglected because what used to be young and developing nations become well-respected superpowers because of the input by the youths. If young people are lazy, the country can be in serious difficulty and there can be no progress. The youth can be the nation's superior force of reckoning, a secret of renaissance, envoys of development, and greatness of a country. They are the shapers of present and future progress because they have the potential, zeal, and energy to give back to their communities when they are well-nourished and employed. The determination and patience of youth will ultimately maneuver the country and put it on the right course to development. Governments and CSOs can play a central role in realizing youth potential through adequate representation and inclusive investment in youth programs and projects.

I understand the circumstances under which young people in South Sudan were raised, however, their dynamism is always homogeneous due to the shared characteristics: energetic, dynamic, innovative, revolutionary, vulnerable, and sometimes naive. Some come from wealthy families, some from low-income families, and some go to school, some do not, some have produced children, some are about to, some live with HIV/AIDS, some care for infected people, some have formal businesses, others do business on the streets, while others are just laborers. But there is a heterogeneous side that includes varying levels of empathy, communication skills, and conflict resolution skills, that differ from one young person to another.

A Passionate Appeal to Youths

The development of young people revolves around the ongoing process of growth, in which all young people strive to satisfy their basic personal and social needs, to be loved, to feel cared for, to be valued, to be beneficial, and to be grounded in spirit, and to build skills and competencies that enable them to function and contribute to nation-building[2]. The principles that I have developed and lived upon over many years inspired me to found the *Nile Youth Development Actions (NYDA)* organization, a grassroots-based catalyst focusing on entrepreneurship, education, employment, and inclusive engagement to promote local socio-economic development in the Nile Basin countries. NYDA was designed to build a solid and unified organization that supports young entrepreneurs in creating jobs in key sectors including agriculture, promoting meaningful training that addresses the current realities of job shortages, and promoting inclusive engagement of young people in co-leadership through a broad intergenerational dialogue. Furthermore, youth development is told in a way that it connotes a process or approach in which young people become competent or develop the skills necessary to succeed and take on challenges.

To have productive youths in South Sudan, we should jointly support the empowerment of young people by involving them in the system, by developing strategies that involve them in nation-building. Youth development should promote conscientiousness, resilience, well-being, and active participation in governance and development processes. The empowerment of the youths is the aftermath of young people, as agents of change, acquiring the skills to influence their own lives and the lives of other individuals, organizations, and communities. Youth empowerment fosters community change, especially in the lives of young people. Active youth participation is a rights-based concept and reaffirms the right of young people to be strengthened as strategic partners in development. Active participation empowers young people to play a decisive role in their personal and community development. It is also asset-based, which speaks to the recognition of young people as key actors in social change, economic growth, and technological innovation.

Some theories of youth participation have been advanced to examine the processes through which young people are involved in development *(DFID/Maguire, S. 2007; Hart,*

---

[2] Benson, P. L., & Pittman, K. J. (Eds.). (2012). Trends in youth development: Visions, realities and challenges (Vol. 6). Springer Science & Business Media.

1992). The important questions that arise concern the nature and quality of participation. Theorists examine whether participation is symbolic or a genuine recognition of the integration of youth into the development process (Hart, 1992). Two theories of youth participation are considered; the Ladder of Youth Participation (Hart, 1992) and the Three Lens Model (World Bank, 2007). The Lens Model for youth participation was adapted from the 2007 World Bank Report that says *"when young people participate meaningfully in the development and implementation of policies and programs that affect them, then services will become effectively tailored to the improvement of their needs"*. The three-lens approach includes involving the youth as beneficiaries, partners, and leaders in development. This approach helps to categorize the current state of development problems and responses to them, to understand whether and how programs, services, and policies appeal to young people.

The *Hart's Ladder* consists of eight rings[3]. In the first, young people are *manipulated*, in the second, young people are *decorated*, while in the third, young people are *symbolized*. In the fourth ring, young people are *assigned and informed*, in the fifth ring they are *consulted and informed*, while in the sixth ring, the decisions initiated by adults are *shared* with young people. In the seventh ring, the young people *lead and initiate actions*, while in the eighth ring the young people and adults *make the decisions together*. Rings 1 and 3 do not provide for youth participation, they may appear as youth participation, but they violate the generally accepted principles of youth involvement. Rings 4-8 indicates the degree of participation of a spectrum of youth involvement efficiency. Within this spectrum, rings 7 and 8 are generally agreed to be the definitive points for effective youth participation.

Roger Hart's *Ladder of Participation* shows young people initiating joint decisions with adults as the top form of participation of young people, followed directly by young people initiating and guiding. This is debatable, an issue for many people who work with and around young people. In essence, the question is which of these levels of participation makes the most sense. Many believe that joint decision-making is most beneficial for both young people and adults. Others believe that young people become

---

[3] Funk, A., Van Borek, N., Taylor, D., Grewal, P., Tzemis, D., & Buxton, J. A. (2012). Climbing the "ladder of participation": engaging experiential youth in a participatory research project. Canadian Journal of Public Health, 103(4), e288-e292.

most empowered when they are making decisions without the influence of an adult. In most cases, this does not exclude adults but reduces their role to be merely supportive. Both arguments have merit; ultimately, it is up to each group to decide which form of decision-making best suits its needs. So which of these models gives you a better understanding of effective youth participation and why? My idea is that young people are better off when they co-lead and make collective decisions with other generations. There needs to be a shift of youth empowerment paradigms to youth investment for self-reliance and sustenance.

In the communities in which young people find themselves, they must be empowered to achieve effective participation and, if necessary, to claim it. Institutions at the state, national, and international levels tend to highlight the most youth participation avenues as being in the *National Youth Union* and the *Ministry of Youth and Sports*. Some stakeholders may be individuals *(young people themselves, role models, or teachers)*. For example, mothers and fathers can be described as *parents* with common interests, while others are youth-based institutions with strong structures including schools, religious institutions, and the media. Political strategies are the most frequently promoted elements for youth participation and all related policies, plans, and schemes for youth development at local, state, national, and international levels.

National Youth Policies, Youth Empowerment Plans, Youth Affirmative Actions, National Development Plans, are some of the operational schemes at the national level that empower youth development. The *African Youth Charter (AYC)* and *Decade Plan of Action (DPOA)* are the continental policies that empower the active involvement of the young people in policy formulation and are at the forefront of strengthening the youth in Africa. These programs are designed to streamline the guidelines and achieve tangible youth-produced results. Programs designed with political support have a stronger footing, as they aim to achieve concrete results, including effective participation of the young people, thus avoiding potential conflicts arising from policy implementation. A clear understanding of key players in young people's participation is essential. What has been presented in this chapter reflects how I envisage a country where young people can engage in dialogue on national issues and be fully involved in the decision-making process in cooperation with other actors.

'Inflated' Bellies

Filled up stomachs at the nation's expense

When we are used to our country's culture, we always answer proudly whenever we are asked how different we are. Harmonious diversity is at times accompanied by the dimensions of race, ethnicity, socio-economic status, age, language, culture, gender, and other ideologies that distinguish people within the social environment. Assuming that the whole world had only one race, one ethnicity, one language, one culture, and one human body trait, wouldn't life have been so monotonous and uninteresting? Or what if your doppelgangers occupied your neighborhood and every day you noticed similar faces, wouldn't it have been a dull sight to you? According to one old saying, everyone has a doppelganger, and there is a perfect duplicate of you nestled somewhere in the world, with your mother's eyes, your father's big nose, and the annoying mole that you always wanted to remove. But how true is this? We live on a planet with almost seven billion people, so surely someone somewhere resembles you. The statement might sound absurd but it carries significant implications, yet the answer is more complicated than you might think.

A few lucky South Sudanese youths, called to public service or engaged in other forms of formal employment have managed to form a common physical trait called *the thick belly*, nourished by regular consumption of expensive wine and alcohol, heavy foods, and for some, recreational drugs. Contrary to this trend, I wish the *millennials* and *Z Generation* exercise more to keep themselves fit and healthy and leave the big-bellies to the *Uncles* and old folks. This does not tantamount to bias against other human natural differences, including visible physical characteristics, personality, and behavior. For example, you may always find both decent and evil people from every race, tribe, religion, and country in various shapes and forms. We just have to harmonize and embrace our cultural differences - as we were all created by God and placed in the Eden of diversity called South Sudan. To achieve a prosperous nation, we must be strivers who focus on enriching the soul, spirit, and mentality, or other

'Inflated' Bellies

individual dispositions to unite the people of the new nation. Forget the body shapes, skin colors, tribal affiliations, religions, or even the fat bellies you notice around in the city because soon I will wage war against such differences so that they are no longer sources of outlandish pride, prosperity, and respect.

For example, if you come across a culture in which men compete for bigger pot bellies or are proud of looking like pregnant women, then you should know that you are in South Sudan. The bloated bellies in this chapter reflect the reality facing almost all South Sudanese youth in politics, the civil service, and those seeking to ascend to a leadership hierarchy. The reality is you don't have to put on such bellies to serve your nation and community, but contrarily, people - young and old, would struggle to have this important symbol for looters and incompetent officials. Bellies represent the corruption syndrome ravaging the soul of South Sudan, as the country is under the charge of inept politicians with protruding bellies of varying shapes and sizes.

Integrity and transparency, guided by a patriotic vision, should end the culture of politicians and civil servants swaggering with big bellies and three smartphones. They should stop deceiving ordinary people with fake pregnancies because their appearance is so disgusting since they never think about going to the gym. My philosophy is that grooming a huge belly is the South Sudanese distinct mark of corruption which is what all civil servants and politicians here share in common. There are also a few corrupt slender guys, but these only eat leftovers from the big corrupt fish's high tables. The painful reality of corruption in South Sudan is that political leaders make deals with foreign companies to advance their selfish interests at the expense of the citizens they swore to serve. That is no different from one official who, before the construction of a new building at one of South Sudan's public universities, imposed conditions that would enable him to secure his *percentage* of funds from the development partners, ignoring the fact that he holds a public office which could jeopardize his conscience in serving the country dutifully.

Corruption is a form of dishonesty perpetrated by the incumbent in public or private institutions, wastefully abusing authority to gain illicit benefits for personal or interest-driven group gains. Corruption in South Sudan involves the misuse of public offices and the abuse of public trust through bribery and embezzlement. Political corruption takes place when an incumbent or other government employee acts in an official capacity for personal enrichment. Corruption is most common in kleptocracies, oligarchies, macro-states, and mafia states. Corruption and veiled criminality are endemic sociological phenomena that take place on a global scale to varying degrees and proportions, and shamefully, South Sudan tops the list of the most corrupt nations. Corruption runs deep in our blood, a critical part of our daily life, and it is like we cannot survive minus engaging in it. Imagine a long line of young aspiring leaders waiting for their turns to plunder state resources and buy villas in foreign countries while showcasing protruding bellies! A recent corruption scandal that went unpunished was the *Juba-Rumbek* road project, part of which was washed away by heavy rainstorms. The effect of corruption in infrastructure is that costs and construction time increase while quality and benefits decrease.

In South Sudan, systemic corruption has incessantly produced temptations, conflicts, discretionary power, monopolistic powers, a lack of transparency, low pay, and a culture of impunity *(as corruption becomes the rule rather than the exception)*. Corruption has been a major issue in South Sudan since the country became autonomous in 2005. Our society is heavily dependent on personal relationships - accompanied by greed for the state wealth, luxuries, and tribal supremacy. Over the last fifteen years, the society has improved its capabilities in the areas of embezzlement, nepotism, smuggling, extortion, favoritism, kickbacks, deception, fraud, waste of public funds, illegal business, stock manipulation, and real estate scams. These social vices have led to excessive poverty, inadequate pay, poor working conditions, and irremediable policies that demoralize people into criminality.

How Corruption Thrives in South Sudan

In South Sudan, the main reason for rampant corruption is the greed for money accumulated by the state, starting from the time when some of our *independence heroes* claimed ownership of the nation and thus dominated all governance structures. Over time, they developed an appetite for endless greed for controlling national resources, portrayed by the malicious accumulation of wealth. Corruption gave way to the monopolization of the political scene by the ruling elite of the *SPLM/A*, who behaved like the hunters and gatherers of the primitive era, except that today they are 'gathering' money, houses, cattle, cars, wives, smartphones, and land. Any appointment for ruling elites is temporary, pending their proven loyalty to a political or military wing leader. Once confirmed, they then embark on uncontrolled looting, stashing money in their second homes within the country, or depositing it in foreign banks where they plan to settle after retirement.

In South Sudan, political monopoly is created by a mixture of guerrilla mentality, village attitude, and political aspirations for supremacy. For most of South Sudan's dominant cattle-raising tribes, seizing and plundering wealth was considered a virtuous prerogative that blended well with the cherished culture of warfare. Envy and desire for other people's success or possessions were widespread, and the violent competition was traditionally the norm. Suppose someone buys a nice suit, his or her brother or friend would go to the same store and buy the same attire or even ask for a better one, regardless of whether it is the right size or not. While many political elites shamelessly misappropriated national resources, other ignorant fighters - riding on their heroic glory of having contributed to the struggle for independence on the battlefield - were made to believe that they deserved to reward themselves with every national resource at their disposal. Nobody could stop them.

The illicit misappropriation of national resources for personal gains started slowly after independence in 2011 and by 2015 it had become so widespread to the extent that it became difficult to keep track of which big man had taken what. Financial scandals involving millions of dollars soon came to light, but nothing was done to curb future embezzlement or corruption, except that no one was arrested because they were all untouchable men and women. If you talked about corruption, the typical reply you were most likely to receive was, *"Where were you when we were fighting? We fought for this country, so we have to eat from it"*. The culture of *the winner takes everything* that has migrated with the *SPLM/A* guerillas from the jungles to the city streets. It had become a zero-sum game, with the corrupt and embezzlers gyrating around public procurement, contracts, construction, road projects, and the combined armed forces. Corruption in South Sudan is thriving, among other factors, due to low levels of civic education, inefficient administrative structures, limited freedom of the press, limited economic freedom, extensive ethnic divisions, and high levels of political predispositions. Other factors include gender inequality, poverty, political instability, low levels of education, lack of engagement with society, and extravagant lifestyles.

The fancy name of *Zoal-Kabier* was coined by the Arabs during the days of unified Sudan to put the Southerners into the margins of the authority by giving them pompous titles and designations to boost the attainment of their short term egos while on the other side exploiting them. The youth should refrain from all these bad, unprogressive rituals that keep our country undeveloped over the years. Why do we have to get drunk while lusting for power when we are incompetent and cannot even meet the expectations of ordinary citizens? Young people should not entertain being called these fanciful names such as *Zola-Khabier, Beny,* and *Kuar Midiit*, etc. These names are deceptive and do not reflect their actual meaning because opportunists use them as a modern tagging style to unwittingly manipulate us. No doubt positions or powers have the potential to drive someone mad in search of arrogant pride.

It is disheartening to witness young people whose aspirations for a better future are based on the assumption of positions and fake titles in various rankings, merely to feed the selfish pursuit of the political ego. In South Sudan, complacency and ego are not reserved exclusively for the young people but are also the root cause for the lack of transparency, accountability, and unethical leadership - features that are unperceivable to the egocentric old politicians. The deep-rooted problems in this country can only be uprooted beginning with asking ourselves the following questions: *Why are things in this country not working as expected? How can we turn around and make things function for the benefit of this country? How can we stop the communal conflicts and tribal politics? How can we fight corruption?*

The very foundations that hold this new nation together are crumbling and the leaders do not care about the looming state collapse, while the common folks do not have the authority nor the competency to do anything to save their country. Whenever we try, the political elites shoot back saying: *Just live your god-forsaken miserable life!* However, I always feel optimistic that, someday we will change the course to which our nation is being steered, though the ongoing events weaken my spirit to the point of believing that nothing can be done to salvage our dear motherland from the widespread destruction the 'freedom' fighters have brought upon it. Nonetheless, it irritates my soul to even think about the dark times that linger ahead unless we push for accountable leadership and active youth involvement in national affairs.

If we let incompetent leadership continue devouring the future of the South Sudanese youths, then we should not expect anything to change. We must willingly embark on the path of national change by taking our small steps for a prosperous and peaceful new nation. Through the *Nile Youth Development Actions (NYDA)*, we are doing our part to develop and promote the subsequent leaders of a better South Sudan who will actively get involved in the country's socio-economic development. To this end, I have participated in many leadership programs across Africa to acquire the competent skills and knowledge essential to bringing about a just and transformative South Sudan for all South Sudanese. My favorite one was the *African Presidential Leadership Program (APLP)* whereupon graduation, I was awarded by *H.E. Abdel Fattah el-Sisi, President of Egypt* and the then Chairperson of the African Union in 2019 as *Africa's Young Promising Leader* alongside four others including *Eric Junior Wagobera* from Uganda, *Sabha Khabsor* from Sudan, *Nada Ibrahim* from Libya, and *Feven Gebremeskel* from Ethiopia. During the program, we envisioned a pro-people leadership to usher in the Africa we all dream of, yearn, fight, and aspire for. We even designed a very engaging policy framework on *Post Conflict Reconstruction and Development (PCRD)*.

My advice to the young South Sudanese is to never take their eyes off the prize as no one should silence them. They should as well avoid the political lifestyles that conform with the old folks who we despise for having failed our country. Shortly after South Sudanese independence, the strong wave of independence swept across the political spectrum, and if you dared to speak the truth, you were countered with false accusations such as being a puppet and an enemy of the state which meant social rejection and avoidance. One South African member of the *African Union Youth Advisory Board* once said that *'when you stand for the truth contrary to the popular falsehoods, then you should be prepared for the dirtiest 'politricks' at your doorstep because you are threatening the big fish's positions and popularity. This is an indicator that ethical and moral leaders are still in want on the continent.*

If we oppose the system, we also question how state institutions continue to function incompetently. We should bear in mind that our demand for change may come at a higher cost, including the loss of life, but the ultimate goal will always remain clear, even to those we quietly inspire, and none of our efforts will go unnoticed. Do not just follow the smooth route by coming in as a politician or military personnel because there are plenty of other means to make a difference and change your society. You just have to find your passion and define your purpose in 21st century South Sudan. What role would you like to play? What nature of footprint do you aspire to leave for generations to come? Do not try to look for areas through which you can fit into the system, because you will jump on the bandwagon and accept to ride along with the status quo you once despised. Rather, we should challenge the norm and become the beacon of hope and calm for the hopeless South Sudanese, as opposed to the hand-picked politicians, who are naturally young but their minds have been adapted to gratify the selfish agenda of their political fathers. Whereas some have realized their mistakes and escaped from the system's tight grip to form new youth-led political parties, others have diminished, collapsed, and relapsed into mainstream politics.

In this context, the booming bellies are a saddening representation of *acute corruption* - the most enduring existential threat to the survival of the Republic of South Sudan. It manifests itself in various dishonest and fraudulent forms, in particular when officials take bribes or allocate public funds to themselves or award contracts to their relatives and associated companies. Because of this repellent behavior, the new nation's government has squandered so many opportunities and resources over the last decade and a half without making tangible progress, even in critical areas like health care, education, agriculture, and intergovernmental physical infrastructure. No sector has suffered more from the wrath of corruption than the oil sector, where prominent figures including oil ministers cause chaos within the oil companies to manipulate and understate the official production figures in barrels per day, while all public tenders are being conducted behind closed doors. This evil conduct empowers them to divert a lot of money from underreported barrels to their accounts. They have had no respect for the rights of oil-producing host communities and states or administrative areas that are politically designed to be independent.

Similar corruption practices have been reported in areas where logging and gold mining take place in the country. If corruption is not tackled directly, it will certainly

'Inflated' Bellies

lead us to permanent instability and ultimately to the balkanization of this young East African country. This is because corruption is a persistent socio-economic and political evil woven in the South Sudanese fabric. If corruption is one blood group, then most people will develop similar tendencies defined by crookedness and that is how it becomes a pandemic that will likely drive our country into the abyss.

During the days of liberation struggles, evils like corruption were dealt with almost instantly by firing squad and this method was very effective. Should South Sudan reintroduce the death penalty for those who engage in the theft of public resources? I believe so, but to a more moderate extent, all corrupt people must be dragged to courts of law and prosecuted accordingly. Where possible, their proceeds of crime should also be confiscated to recover the plundered public resources. Several of the country's most powerful politicians and generals appear to have amassed illegitimate wealth in the decade that followed the signing of the *Comprehensive Peace Agreement* in 2005 *(which ended the North-South War and laid the ground for a referendum that led to South Sudan's independence)*. Much of the wealth these leaders amassed was from a high-end real estate outside the country and large commercial stakes in both the public sector and oil services contracted in South Sudan. South Sudanese law makes it illegal for the holders of constitutional office to conduct business outside the government while in office. The *SPLA Act of 2009* prohibits nepotism and corrupt practices by all *SPLM/A* employees and makes such activities punishable by a lengthy prison sentence. So how is this systemic corruption institutionalized?

Tackling Corruption in South Sudan

Tackling corruption in South Sudan requires a holistic and systemic approach that includes the ratification of both regional and international treaties in corruption like the *African Union Convention to Prevent and Combat Corruption (AUCPCC)*, the *OECD Anti-Bribery Convention*, and the *UN Convention Against Corruption*. Not only that but there must be prompt investigations followed by prosecution, and sanctions against anyone found guilty of corruption. We also need to develop minimum standards and practical guidelines for ethical procurement and introduce open procurement practices to make data clearer, easier to analyze, and accessible to the public. Public complaints must be collected and treated confidentially to promote anonymous reporting of all cases of corruption. The media should also be involved in the fight against corruption, while civil society organizations must be empowered to hold the government and its leadership answerable on behalf of the public.

It is worth noting that regional and international bureaucrats have worked hand in hand with South Sudan's leadership to abet corruption, state capture, and civil war. If we want concrete reforms, we must also freeze all undeclared accounts held abroad in banks, serving politicians and government officials. The state should also impose travel sanctions, lifelong bans from holding public office, denial of access to luxury goods and real estate abroad while calling upon foreign governments to investigate the illegal flow of money used to finance atrocities here and buy palatial homes abroad. To achieve this, we must encourage and support South Sudan's efforts in combating the laundering of assets looted from the state coffers and by imposing asset freezes on those responsible for human rights violations and financial misconduct.

Regional governments and financial institutions must play a leading role in combating the laundering of assets looted from South Sudan. The majority of assets belonging to South Sudan's top officials mentioned in many investigative reports are located in South Sudan's neighbors like Kenya, Uganda, and Ethiopia. Moreover, the governments of these countries can decide to act on our behalf and help us recover these properties. These governments should therefore freeze and seize the assets belonging to the top South Sudanese officials who are collectively responsible for the never-ending atrocities, financial embezzlement, corruption, as well as violating the peace agreements signed in August 2015 and September 2018.

The banks where our stolen money is stashed need to consider taking proactive attempts to block these individuals' accounts where the money is kept. Banks may also decide that it is too risky for them to conduct any financial transactions with South Sudanese account holders which can help prevent money laundering or illegal money transfers abroad. To ensure that banks do not cut off all businesses in their effort to prevent the laundering of corrupt proceeds out of South Sudan, financial monitoring mechanisms need to be established to issue advisories to the banking community stressing proper banking procedures with clear financial records for their customers. The South Sudanese leadership, with technical and advisory support from the regional and international community, should establish a supervisory mechanism for the collection of revenues, budgets, revenue allocation, and government expenditure. Despite the peace agreement being stern on the abuse of public treasures and the conceited lip service by South Sudanese leaders, the government has failed to implement constructive fiscal management practices. Given the severity of the economic crisis in South Sudan and the urgent need for external funding, international donors may now have the opportunity and leverage to push for greater financial oversight and accountability over how their donor funds are spent.

Determining the special mechanism of external supervision for any additional financial resources requires concessions and considerable diplomatic state-level engagement, especially in the light of potential concerns about the violation of sovereignty. It was clear from the various consultations that the absence of equitable resource allocation and consequent marginalization of the various groups in South Sudan was a simmering source of resentment and disappointment underlying the conflagration that ensued, albeit the implosion of the conflict was brought about by the political struggle by the two main players *(main SPLM vs SPLM-IO)*.

The struggle for political power and control over natural resource revenues, corruption, and nepotism appear to be the contributing factors in the outbreak of the crisis that devastated the entire country. But we shouldn't deceive ourselves: the current war is not about a change of system in South Sudan but is a war between the political and military elites trying to gain control of South Sudan and plunder its resources. *"An estimated $4 billion remains unaccounted for, and it is feared it was stolen by former and current corrupt officials with close ties to government officials,"* President Kiir wrote in a letter to government officials leaked to the press in June 2012. But these funds have never been recovered, and the kleptocratic system that made looting possible in the first place is entirely intact. The *2009 Anti-Corruption Commission Act* and the *2011 Transitional Constitution* require senior officials, including the president, to disclose their income, assets, and liabilities, including those of their spouses and children. However, no public official has ever come out to do so for the last fifteen years.

In July 2020, the Subcommittee of the Economic Cluster of the *Revitalized Transitional Government of National Unity (R-TGoNU)* conducted investigations on all revenue collection points to assess the amount of public money being collected and how revenues are remitted into the national treasury. In its preliminary findings, the committee stated that import taxes among others are still being channeled into the public account. It called for a thorough investigation into the theft of non-oil revenues, which are believed to have been siphoned off from the official public account. Many customs officials have also accused their bosses of grave misconduct, leading to reduced revenues. All non-oil revenue is by law wired into the account of the *National Revenue Authority (NRA)* mandated to assess, collect, manage, and enforce tax and revenue-related laws. Domestically, weak state institutions have failed to check corruption and the movement of ill-gotten gains out of the country, a remarkable failure that our government has stopped short of resolving.

The fight against corruption in South Sudan requires both the adoption and enforcement of a comprehensive legal framework, the strengthening of its state institutions, and ensuring accountable processes for public procurement, licensing, and financial management. The establishment of public registers to report corrupt officials, inefficient companies, or state institutions will also stimulate public involvement in the fight against corruption. The government must also protect whistleblowers and support civil and political rights while working with other nations to investigate and combat corruption. High priority should be given to major corruption cases involving politicians and senior public officials, which have serious corrosive political and social consequences such as blocking the attainment of the *UN Sustainable Development Goals*. Finally, the millions in money flowing from South Sudan pass through financial systems that end somewhere in Europe. Our government must try to work with countries where our stolen money is destined so that corruption is fought on both sides. This may include making arrangements for the swift, transparent, and accountable return of assets and other ill-gotten resources that we can use to develop our nation.

Social Vices and Rituals

Iniquities eating up the new nation!

Every society has some distinct traditions and rituals that determine the way of life of the local people. In Ethiopia, people eat minced raw beef *(Kitfo)* as part of a subculture alongside other customs such as drinking coffee *(Buna)* during festivities. Gosh! To this day, I am still in love with *Habesha Buna (coffee-making ceremony)*. Over the *Buna*, discussions about anything on life can be held, and dealings are sealed. I remember participating in *Habesha Buna* during class intervals while undertaking my Mining Engineering degree program at Unity University in Addis Ababa. I met decent people in the *Buna* bars, such as *Misgana Gebre Michael*, my best friend, from university in the teeming city of Addis Ababa that is full of the hustle and bustle of everyday life. Comparatively, the South Sudanese have a habit of sitting for hours under trees in traditional tea places, sometimes harboring unemployed youth who waste away their energy in the negativity that will never yield fruitful results or transform South Sudan. Other irritating South Sudanese habits include practicing witchcraft and quarreling over trivial matters and smoking *hookah/shisha*.

My brother and sister, while you are busy wasting your precious time on irrelevant matters, in other countries the youth are the driving force behind the national transformation, and so we must wake up from our lazy slumber and build our nation to catch up with the rest of the world. The lack of job opportunities is one of the huge unresolved problems beleaguering the African continent, with unemployment among the youths standing at 60%, according to the World Bank's 2017 report. Being out of work makes our young people vulnerable to the evils of corruption, civil conflict, immorality, and counterfeiting that are becoming the new normal. Our incompetent leadership has made it tough for the South Sudanese youths to achieve their full productivity potential as they are denied access to job opportunities as they have also failed to create empower them to become self-employed.

Long-held primitive policies have also let the youths down, especially when the old pot-bellied folks taunt them with scornful remarks like *"It is who you know"* and these have demoralized our youths. Other unpleasant habits include the pressure of materialism, which drives our young people mad because they cannot afford luxurious items such as clothes, shoes/sneakers, watches, jewelry, hair wigs, skin lightening creams, smartphones, and cars. This social pressure drives them into wanton criminality and violence. Nevertheless, I have seen many South Sudanese youth dress so fashionably, elegantly, and ostentatiously all the time, which makes it difficult for anyone to understand their real plight, as it is impossible to distinguish between the rich and poor as they all follow the same luxurious lifestyle. All they do is to appear elegant in their expensive suits and red ties, sitting idly under the trees, drinking tea, and talking about how the country is being badly governed, while simultaneously praising and defending their political demigods, and how they wear the same suit brands like them. Young people are excessively anxious about their inability to afford the things they admire most, and all they think about is acquiring them illegally, as their political demigods have always done. This lowers their morale, self-esteem, while materialistic stress and social bullying keep increasing.

Today's society teaches our young people that owning expensive branded goods gives them a higher social prestige in their community and that they are better than anyone else who cannot afford such luxury. Can you see how mentally ill South Sudanese flashy culture has become? They believe a materialistic life is the best way to enjoy life to the fullest. From experience, entering this profligate life diverted many young people from moral values to immoral activities, including chasing after sugar daddies, sugar mamas, and engaging in commercial sex. Some rich guys have made a habit of luring the youth into sexual overactivity, which is a disgusting reality of modern life. Beneath this lecherous life lies deadly poisons, such as accumulating debt, misery, and a culture of excessive begging by young people desperate to fund their luxurious lifestyles. The *Uncles* in expensive suits and red ties have done much harm in keeping the desperate young people in this never-ending cycle of begging and wasteful spending.

I know, however, of some dignified young people who can never be tempted to adopt such offensive and greedy lifestyles simply because their dignity and morality are their pride. Some may argue with my narrative, calling all these behaviors vital and normal, but I acknowledge those who deserve respect, and I applaud the people who enjoy serving the community, such as the farmers who send their vegetables to the local market, a teacher who goes to school every morning, and a garbage collector who knocks on your door to take your trash for proper disposal. These are the earnest income-generating ventures that must be valued and appreciated. So dear South Sudanese youth, contribute to the development of society and not just your stomach or bragging about the branded suits you ordered from Dubai. Luxuries do not matter in building an indomitable nation! We need our young people to stay healthy, educated, employed, and safe to appreciate this short-lived life and not waste it away.

Why not re-evaluate our selection of people who influence us? A great motivational speaker Jim Rohn once said, *"You are the average of the five people you spend the most time with"*, all of them with their material needs, sense of humor, goals, and plans. Of course, people with acceptable moral conduct, responsible and successful, can be a positive force in our lives. We better not pile more pressure on our poor fathers who are still struggling to feed us, yet we are already-fit to work with our two hands and two legs. The individual must carefully select his/her peers who model fruitful ideas, behaviors, habits, and rightful rituals. We must let go of the materialistic cultures that are deeply rooted in our genes and exist in every South Sudanese family, including our own piddling, hated, and beloved social blocs. But what happens when these practices are no longer *normal* and *logical*? That is how rituals become manifested by people's bizarre beliefs and the once-entrenched and tamed practices become a strange cultic phenomenon and a barrier to social growth. Conflict and instability persist throughout the country, as the main cause of this disease of unproductivity and professional dormancy. The lack of patriotism among the South Sudanese youth is another grave ritual that must be replaced by the imposition of national values that put South Sudan at the forefront of issues to create an inclusive atmosphere where people have fair access to equal opportunities.

After decades of the liberation struggle, the country is once again in the middle of a devastating conflict raging on since 2013 *(The SPLM House Downfall)*. Many believe the key factor contributing to this is the lack of a deep collective identity or a common sense of nationality. The possibility of becoming a nation stems in part from having a common history, culture, and identity while at the same time deepening the understanding of the shared values of cultural diversity and learning to live together with tolerance and harmony. Both the political leaders and ordinary citizens must recognize the significance of national unity and the appropriate demonstration and celebration of cultural diversity as a national treasure. However, cultural pluralism in South Sudan is poorly handled as the most obvious obstacle to national cohesion is the exclusion of some tribes from the national platform, particularly along ethnic lines and tribal bias. There is an urgent need for our academic system to integrate the different cultures of South Sudan in the national curriculum through folktales, musical instruments, hunting spears, cooking pots, symbols, traditional customs and songs, and to celebrate the shared heritage together.

Disowning Blackness

Our females are attuned to burping habits that are not part of our natural being, not only among millennials or adolescents but also older women. Recently, I met a 50-year-old woman who explained to me that whitening cream is an integral part of her life, even as she gets older and can't move, her children will apply the cream to her body, she said. I don't know from where she came with this philosophy but I consider that to be an irrational belief. I think that if there is a possibility, she will even apply the same cream to her graveyard. I know many make jokes out of it, some say the creams make their faces look like *Mirinda* and their legs like *Coca-Cola* bottles, thus symbolizing how the creams deform the human body - the face will usually appear yellow, brown, or something of that sort, while the legs disgustingly remain black. Fake guys are deceived and attracted by these phony appearances, but the whole trend irritates me a lot because the person applying these creams is made to appear like a burn survivor. A lack of appreciation of cultures and diversity is evident in a young generation that believes their culture is the supremest and all-important in South Sudan. I implore us to embrace our blackness and try not to change what God gifted us as no culture is superior to the other. From the same perspective, I propose an annual culture appreciation day to remind ourselves of the beauty of our cultural lifestyles including appearances, as this can be an excellent reminder of the importance of cultural diversity as a driving force for tolerance and inter-societal development.

The Generation of Facebook and Instagram

The Facebook and Instagram generation in this section imply the digital/dot com millennials born after 1994. Due to the influence of Facebook and Instagram in their lives, they are difficult to raise, manage, and are seen as being self-centered, unfocused, and indolent. The conveniences of modern life have spawned a lazy generation who have grown up with low self-esteem, living a double-standard life that can be evident in the world of immense beauty filters on Facebook and Instagram. These filters are only good at portraying people in a kind of amazing life that is perceived in their altered faces, which also hide the depressed and miserable lives they secretly live behind the curtains. They complement this by providing false and boastful information including having studied at the *University of Oxford, Harvard University, University of Cambridge,* or living in *New York* or *London* to give a deceptive pretense to their perceived lavish living. The perception is disgusting, but they just numb themselves without having any idea of what they are putting themselves in.

The technology that creates a constant engagement with social media via flashy smartphones releases a harmful invisible 'chemical' for temporary happiness which is like getting a text, feeling good about it, but without it, you are lonely, upset, and depressed. It is as if their lives become worthy only when their photos get more views, likes, comments, and shares, which gives them ultimate satisfaction. However, when their photos get fewer likes, comments, views, and shares than expected, they feel worthless and dejected which gets worse when they are blocked or simply ignored by those they believed were their online friends. There are also some unpleasant addictive behaviors including smoking, alcohol, drug use, gambling, and other harmful mind-altering substances which provide them with relief from stress.

The involvement of any young person in the above behavioral trends depends heavily on the kind of influence of his/her peers, co-workers, and the people with whom he or she is connected, who have the potential to either renew or ruin his or her entire life. There is no deep, meaningful relationship in which someone can turn to a real-world friend for advice and guidance, but they simply turn to social media and a bottle of alcohol to escape the distressing adolescence as coping mechanisms. Young people who spend most of their time on social media are more depressed than those who have less access to or access to it to earn money and professionalism. Don't get me wrong: social media is instrumental in improving connectivity across geographical barriers, but failure to properly control yourself while using it is a trap. While gambling is fun, but too much of it is dangerous and alcohol is not bad either, but drinking a lot of it uncontrollably is reckless, irresponsible, and disrespectful. Owning a smartphone is neither bad, but too much of it will get you lost in the virtual world where immorality, indecency, and ignoring your family becomes the new norm.

Addiction to smartphones also sets a dangerous precedent. If you are sitting at a meeting, or a family dinner with people you are supposed to be interacting with but instead you are always busy with your smartphone, then this small act is a huge insult to your colleagues, work colleagues, or even family members. It shows that you are not interested in the meeting as it is not your top priority at the moment. The fact that you can't put your phone down during such a critical time is a sign of a deep-rooted addiction - if you wake up and check your phone before saying good morning to your spouse, roommate, or friend next to you, you are seriously addicted. Like other forms of addiction, smartphone addiction can potentially ruin your relationship by robbing you of quality family time, gobbling up your money, and lowering the quality of your life. Consequently, we have a generation raised with less self-esteem and no adequate coping mechanism to deal with social stress in life. And these are our future leaders?

Besides, patience is an unknown phenomenon among young people who want to run right after birth. Anxiety has engulfed the young Facebook and Instagram generation who always want everything 'right now' while despising the natural processes. They know nothing about social coping mechanisms like job satisfaction and the contentment that comes from maintaining close-knit real-life relationships as there are no specific *apps* for all of that. These social skills are only learned in real life through physical interactions, away from the influence of social media. But it only takes dedicated, selfless, caring people to understand the importance of physical interactions, in contrast to online interactions. Without any real-life experience, young people forget that this life is like climbing a mountain - whether you climb it faster or slower, it remains a mountain as the distance to the peak remains the same, so we must always ascend starting from the base.

We need to learn and practice to be patient, especially concerning things that are important including love, job fulfillment, and joy; love of life, self-confidence, and earning professional qualifications to have teeming successful careers. All this requires endurance and hard work because the road ahead of each one of us is long and bumpy. To successfully climb the mountain, you need to start asking for directions, be guided by the more experienced people, while keeping your focus on reaching the summit as efficiently as [possible. The worst-case scenario is giving up halfway through, resulting in suicides, and excessive drug and alcohol abuse.

Common Rituals

Some aspects of South Sudan's traditional culture have eroded over time. The advances of modern society, including improved communication, opportunities for greater social and economic mobility, and the spread of a monetary economy, as well as decades of war and human displacement, have led to a general loosening of social ties, customs, relationships, and modes of organization in traditional cultures. Yet much of the past remains intact. One of the most important ancient forms of cultural expression in South Sudan has always been the oral communication method. Folklore and myths, as well as the retelling of history and traditions, have always been passed down from one generation onto the next. It is also through oral means that advice, guidance, and knowledge for dealing with typical life problems were delivered. Many South Sudanese groups use ritual and ceremonial practices to mark the stages in the life cycle of the individual - birth, circumcision, puberty, marriage, and death. Facial scarring and tattooing as methods of ritual ornament are widespread throughout the country. Most social groups have a patrilineal lineage, but the importance of such connections among related groups varies from one community to another[4]. Polygamy is practiced in some social groups and is considered a means of expanding affiliate *(in-law)* relationships and obtaining social support. Although divorces are common today, a broken marriage was considered a disgrace in the past because it destroyed the fabric of relationships. Most groups historically had some form of social class distinction but these have gradually faded over time.

---

[4] https://worldreliefmemphis.org/south-sudan-cultural-profile

Should the people of South Sudan decide to seriously abdicate the issues of political identity, then either the spirit of nationalism should be left to the political elite, or the people will need to find a new way of divorcing politics from the state. We cannot underestimate the need for involving people from all the four corners of South Sudan represented by their legislative assembly members, the council of states, and participation of special interest groups including women, youths, the private sector, and religious leaders. A resolution like this can dismantle the impression that the *SPLM/A* owns South Sudan and give its political elites the upper hand in abusing state resources by squandering every cent in the state coffers. In *July 2011*, I was among the excited people waving the flag of independence as we marched to the *Freedom Square* in Juba to celebrate with the tens of thousands of others who were thrilled at the prospect of a new life and a new beginning in the new nation of South Sudan. Only three years later, the joy for the hard-won self-governance was cut short by the *Oyee*[1] Party's shortfalls which ignited a fire within their internal affairs in 2013 and escalated to devastate the whole country. These actions forced half of the population to seek refuge in the *United Nations Protection of Civilians' (POCs)* sites while others had to flee to refugee camps in the different neighboring countries for safety.

Until then, I had learned that peace is not simply a choice, but a prerequisite for our very existence in this world. The absence of it breeds unspeakable tragedies and dismay. As such, every South Sudanese should embrace peace, beginning with oneself and then externally triggering it in love, laughter, and harmony. Living in South Sudan may never be an *American Dream* to some people's standards due to a myriad of unresolved differences that still keep haunting us. During the struggle for a new nation, I repeatedly heard the distressing sounds of gunshots being recklessly fired followed by the dreadful screams of desperate people fleeing their burnt down villages and running away into the unknown; an experience that I do not wish for anyone. Now, in my youthfulness, a similar scenario is playing out, and it is even much worse considering that the young people are the most enticed into this endless culture of violence and revenge. No one seems worried about the mindless loss of life, and the collapse of the economy - a terrible reality that we live in today.

---

[1] Oyee is a political term that is used to motivate crowds.

Demilitarizing Our Mindsets

Towards an inclusive and progressive South Sudan!

On one particular day in *August 2019*, children from our neighborhood streamed into our compound to play, and thereafter retreated under a massive shady tree to escape the scorching heat of the Juba sun. As was the norm, they built mini-houses from clay – rendering their future architectural masterpiece. Then they assembled humans totting with guns. Just as they were playing, one kid charged in walking in an imaginary gun-toting posture accompanying it with imitated gunshot sounds. Upon the imaginary sense of danger, the children who were stationed in their mini house reacted quickly to repel the shooter with their imaginary machine guns complemented by the imitated sounds of RPG shots. Just imagine a 4-year-old child, aware of the vulnerability of his community/country, believes that he must defend his homestead against marauding gunmen who have since kept the country restless with uncontrolled violence, looting, murder, rape, and intimidation.

Thus, most children in South Sudan have been raised in a war-mongering environment while some millennials have not only been victims of war but have actively fought in wars as child soldier recruits. Since many fought in the liberation war during their early teens, they are familiar with the sights and sounds of machine guns and hence are well aware of the devastation caused by wars. I grew up in a similar environment, not any different from the millions of other young people who are pressured into joining militant groups with promises of security, a sense of belonging, and seizing anything in their way, without regard for the needy just as the *SPLM/A* did during the liberation struggles. At times, they attributed this ruthlessness to the spirit of the national struggle, but the forcible recruitment of child soldiers is a heinous act of child abuse, and some *SPLM/A* war commanders did so for reasons best known to them.

In April 2014, the *United Nations Human Rights* Chief *Mrs. Navi Pillay* reported that more than 9,000 child soldiers have been fighting in South Sudan's civil war, with forceful recruitment by both the army and rebel forces. These figures include children with armed groups, children who wear military uniforms and carry weapons, and children who receive military training in another part of the country. This is not the kind of South Sudan that we all hoped for when we trooped to vote in the referendum – it is the opposite of the country on which our sustenance and dreams depend. Militarized politically-minded warlords emphatically train child soldiers on how to kill fellow humans whose tribes are different from theirs. However, it should be noted that the warlords' children are being sent abroad to live a luxurious life, receive the best education, and later be appointed to work in diplomatic missions. It is only the children from poor families who are targeted instead of the militarized politically-minded warlords' children.

Rather than fighting each other in the jungle, vulnerable South Sudanese children must be sent to school to learn how to contribute appropriately to their country's development, in particular, by addressing the need for achieving the *Sustainable Development Goals (SDGs)*. Instead of being trained to be warriors, violent criminals, and warmongers, our children must be trained to be admirable pilots, outstanding engineers, esteemed doctors, and proud astronauts. It is saddening that in the new nation, children are learning to clean and assemble machine guns as they prepare for the next deadly attack or ambush in the jungles of their native South Sudan. These child soldiers have been part of the problem that the new nation has faced through endless internal violent conflicts since 2013 except for the period between the 2019 ceasefire agreement and the formation of the *R-TGoNU* in February 2020.

The relapse to square one, which is always accompanied by violence and the destruction of people's livelihoods as the country experienced in 2016, is always predictable. The rapid retrogression into chaos was caused by the failure of the *SPLM/A* in 2011 after independence to transform the liberation movements, particularly the then military wing of *SPLM* into a professional army that protects the sovereignty of the nation and free from political ideologies – even after renaming it to *South Sudan Peoples' Defense Force (SSPDF)*. In the transitional phase, the divorced

*SPLM/A*s can transform themselves into dynamic governing parties and not as the pot-bellied *Uncles* who aimlessly roam the cities in military fatigue when things get out of hand. Such sights only implore the minds of young people into joining militant groups. In South Sudan, it is common to come across a political figure who refers to himself as a Military General, an Honorable Member of Parliament, and an Executive Member of the Cabinet! But all for what? Just intimidation!

The trend of transformation would be more successful in establishing pluralistic democratic societies that can pave the way for political parties to advocate for reforms, engage in political discourses while promoting sustainable development, rather than being a stumbling block to democratic dispensation and eternal peace. A clear distinction must be made between politics and the state, it should be stressed that the *SPLM/A* is not South Sudan and South Sudan is not the *SPLM/A*. One political party can govern for a while, and others can have the same opportunity *(if democratically elected)* to govern the country, but South Sudan remains the same, no matter which political party is in charge. Similarly, the military should be transformed into a disciplined national army that pledges allegiance to the civilian government, regardless of the ruling political party. The national military implements the provisions of the security chapter of the revived 2018 peace agreement through a merger that brought together the militaries of all warring parties - the procedures that will last until the end of the transition period in 2023.

The name *Sudan People's Liberation Army* will in the meantime be changed to *South Sudan Peoples' Defense Forces*. We need to do more in logical reasoning than simply changing the name, because those who sacrifice themselves to be in the military should be called patriots or loyalists and not indisciplined armed men, warlords, and conflict-mongers who are intent on looting, pillaging, killing, and raping. If possible, I am willing to send a few selected military combatants for further training to acquire competent expertise that can help reintegrate them into civilian life. Nevertheless, it is essential for South Sudan and its people to put aside all detrimental injustices and work hand-in-hand towards inclusive strategic guidelines to meet the challenges of a sustainable transition from war to peace and to prevent relapses into another wave of endless conflicts, even when elections are imminent.

One Monday morning in September 2011, three months after independence, I came across a field where students were playing football in *Midaan Simba (Simba Square)* during school hours. By then, I was working at Custom Market selling different kinds of recorded music. Along the way, I saw some children playing in the road, and the first thing that came to my mind was that *'these children must be at school instead of playing in the streets at this time'*. I asked their chaperon Lado, "Why aren't you in class?", and he replied, "*Bleed Da Ma B'e Sheahadaad*" which loosely translates to mean *this country is not liberated by certificates*. His response implied that education in South Sudan was irrelevant to him and his colleagues, a line from a new song by *Garang Ateny*, a renowned artist who praised the *SPLM/A* for liberating the country with guns. However, the artist may have forgotten that the *SPLM/A* founder *Dr. John Garang De Mabior* was a Ph.D. holder at a top American university.

This culture of advocating for a military mindset across the country is explained and correctly identified by the current Minister for Peace in the R-TGoNU, *Hon. Stephen Par Kuol*, who said in one of his published articles that to achieve peace in South Sudan, we should give priority to the culture of opting for peace over wars. Due to the lack of holistic *Post-Conflict Reconstruction and Development (PCRD)* and the utilization of Early Warning and Response Mechanisms, in December 2013 South Sudan relapsed into a deadly conflict that resulted in the death of thousands of lives, as well as causing mass displacement of over 2.2 million civilians to the neighboring countries, severe hunger, and economic meltdown. Since then, the *'gun culture'* has brought about untold suffering to the new nation through politicized tribal warfare, inter-communal revenge killings, and cattle raiding.

It is not the weapon, but rather, the violence-possessed spirits and souls behind the destructive weapons that devastated precious lives, burned down villages, and cast the vulnerable orphans onto all the streets of South Sudan. The long history of armed struggle with Sudan and the subsequent armed resistance after independence created opportunities for the proliferation of weapons and the recruitment of militia groups. Militia groups have recruited tens of thousands of young people who are neither working nor going to school, ostensibly to protect the lives of warlords and their cattle, wives and political leaders from danger. They fight with heavy machine guns not only in war with the state, but also in inter-communal conflicts, often triggered

Demilitarizing Our Mindsets

by raiding kraals and taking off with cattle for dowry payment, theft of household items, and kidnapping of young girls to take as wives. Political elites often tolerated Armed and militia groups and co-operated when needed to realize the military and political objectives of those striving for power. In other words, it was precisely the violence in our political minds and the rampage under the command of political warlords that led South Sudan to its knees. Blaming guns will not help because weapons do not choose who to kill, but their owners, and this debate won't help in ending violence in the country. Therefore, guns don't kill people, rather, they are the wrongly militarized people who choose to misuse the guns and kill people at will. The war-minded political elites believe that every problem must be solved by fighting each other and believing that they must trade with war as a means to earn a living.

The country is wrongly steered onto the path of violence and widespread destruction, which is politically institutionalized because the ringleaders of the splintered SPLM/A publicly advocate joining the militia while calling for widespread destruction and a militarized spirit that only knows how to kill a supposed enemy of its military commander. It is the same incitement that has been instilled among the guerrillas since 1983 and has since then engraved the culture of violence into political struggles – the culture of *we* and *you* of separatists and unionists, of the New Sudan and the New Republic in the South. All these political uncertainties have hampered the unity of the people of South Sudan for decades, and it was the same centrifugal force for the outbreak of conflict in 2013. It will likely be the same catalyst for all future conflicts if the current paradigm continues to gain momentum.

A politician once told me to get military training so that I could get a job in government or senior positions in the *tribalized* oil companies which are habitually obtained through political endorsements or bribery rather than through transparent and equitable means. Illiterates rule this country. So deeply entangled are our current generation in irreversible violence and a militarized spirit. I wonder why I should join the military to work professionally with my hard-earned academic qualifications in engineering. Screw you! I am a professional rebel of ideas and I will not buy this cheap advice, I know where I will be working untiringly for my life. Our politicians are military-minded people who only turn to fight with weapons to settle their disputes, and it would be no surprise if our politicians pass onto the next generation their violence-inspired fantasies because that is where their interests and priorities lie. Most politicians encourage young people to join the army to defend their selfish interests and sometimes they use their constitutional authority to coerce the local youths who are against military service. That is how the savage military generals in uniforms are turning guns against innocent people and killing them mercilessly.

In the words of *Hon. Stephen Par Kuol*, civility, is therefore not part of the vocabulary of our political discourse. Militarism is glorified in every situation, and it is only in South Sudan where civilian politicians assume military ranks and wear military uniforms as if they are badges of honor. Remarkably, the civilian population in the countryside is highly armed and militarized. Weapons and violence give young men in this civilian army community a revered sense of masculinity and you cannot be a total man without possessing a gun. *Honorable Kuol* emphasized his call for millennials to rise-up and face the challenges of the decade in replacing the warmongering *liberation dinosaurs* who made corruption the new face of politics in South Sudan.

Kuol reiterated that the squandering of public resources without accountability, the *'my turn of eating'* philosophy that derails the economy to hell with rampant inflation, must ultimately be stopped by enlightened new young leaders. The political history of many African countries is often associated with the armed struggle for freedom and independence, and these narratives support the widespread belief that violence is the indispensable weapon for achieving freedom from foreign subjugation, but the South Sudanese are instead pointing their weapons into one another. These narratives imply that the power and historical role of nonviolent civil resistance in the quest for liberation is ignored. Henceforth, the narratives of violence have overshadowed the history and potential of nonviolent action in South Sudan.

The number one enemies of the state are the incumbent *Uncles* in red ties who tribalized the political atmosphere in South Sudan. Civil society, labeled by the state as *traitors* play a major role in silencing the weapons to create a peaceful environment in which different communities can correspond with each other while discussing issues that affect both of them. Similarly, former warring parties should join forces to develop opportunities by exploring their common need to prevent conflict and revenge killings. I hope that the youth of today, who are the next generation, will

Demilitarizing Our Mindsets

continue the intertribal engagements, awareness-raising campaigns on the dangers of crime and violence prevention, to foster a non-violent society, while simultaneously making the local population aware of the villainous intentions of the incumbent pot-bellied *Uncles* in red ties and black suits. Whoever seeks to bring about change in South Sudan must be sure that his mind is not militarized. This does not mean that the author comes from a relatively calm environment without a history of injuries, pain, or trauma. I have experienced many violent wars, the shock still haunts me, but my logic is that we cannot confront violence with violence. When we have good intentions, we should mean peace, and we must seek peaceful means of conflict resolution and co-existence.

The challenge is that even if we know and have lived the exact opposite of peace, have survived our struggles, and want to help, we can still bring a belligerent mindset to healing. A warlike mindset will not produce a cure but instead will prolong confusion, and when people are confused they tend to do whatever they wish, even if it is not what they need. For us to not bring confusion to the healing work we do, it is imperative that we continually ensure that our mindset is a demilitarized and neutral zone where peace dwells, is nurtured, and shared. Our mind's zone is truly within our full control regardless of any extenuating external circumstances. As humanity, we will not know peace until we first know it within our minds.

The challenge is that people always want peace, but they *(especially the young people)* allow others to heavily corrupt and militarize their minds to always attack or defend, while simultaneously considering other ways of furthering this cycle vis-à-vis the supposed enemy. What if the entire lifespan of a militarized spirit is the enemy, not just our own, but an evil dictator who is ruining our progress as human beings? Military thoughts produce martial language, which ultimately leads to the reality of war. If we want peace, we must be aware that peace is also a reality - a reality that begins in our thoughts. When we hear talk and rumors of peace, we should be confident that it will ultimately become a reality of peace. In a demilitarized spirit, you will not allow others to harbor weapons of mass destruction such as unfounded gossip, fabricated malice, prejudice, discrimination, unhealthy thoughts, and clumsy desires.

Within the gardens of a demilitarized mind exists appreciative inquiry, respect, patience, compassion, empathy, awareness, and love. A militarized mind will press the panic button and declare either an emergency lockdown or a full-scale attack because of disagreements and views. A demilitarized mind knows that differing opinions are wonderful and need neither attack nor defense, and capitulation to the views of another is never expected because this happens only during war. A demilitarized mind is not interested in being right, but in understanding and reaching a compromise. Misunderstandings are missed opportunities for cultivating peace, and therefore listening from the heart will awaken a language of humanity, sympathy, and genuine discourse, not monologues.

In a demilitarized zone, our engagements with others will not be discussions and plans for slander, accusations, strife, defense, and attack. Our discourses will focus on lasting solutions, affinities, and how we can put our differences together like arranging the various pieces of a jigsaw puzzle to create a beautiful picture. Each of us holds different pieces, but no piece is less necessary or less significant than the other. For those who truly want peace, now is the time to demilitarize our inner thought processes and allow peace to prevail within us, our families, communities, and nation.

Demilitarization is a multidimensional process that involves reversing militarization by sustainably reducing the size and influence of the military sector in the state and society, and redistributing military resources in the civilian process. It seeks to deconstruct the cultural, ideological, and institutional structures of militarism. My focus in this chapter is on the demilitarization of society, which goes hand in hand with the deglorification of the armed forces by the media and society in general. A favorable internal environment is characterized by a low incidence of violent inter-factional conflict, a functioning law enforcement system, the considerable political will to plan and implement demilitarization policies, and public support for such efforts, including the media. Militarism is said to exist when symbols, values, and discourses validating military power and preparation for war are prevalent in the society, such as what took place in December 2013 *(SPLM's House Downfall)*. It embodies the belief that a nation's power lies primarily, if not exclusively, in its military strength. The first is a process that contributes to militarism, namely the excessive use and abuse of force plus the mounting importance of militarist ideologies, values, and beliefs about human nature and social relations which are influenced by the ruling party in the sphere of power. The second is marked by increasing military spending, the size of the armed forces, and arms imports and production. It is also characterized by the increasing demands of the military on society and the economy, and consequently by the possible increase in the political role and influence of the military and its actual appropriation of the state apparatus.

The demilitarization of South Sudan's society is largely uncharted territory - surprising, given the open militarization process which the South Sudanese society is likely to undergo from 2020 to 2023. Under the *SPLM/A*'s rule, the military is a pervasive force blocking the country's education system. Currently, the media, particularly the state-owned *South Sudan Broadcasting Corporation (SSBC)*, newspapers, radio broadcasters, and television stations, openly condoned violence as a legitimate means of brutally dealing with the opposition while supporting the use of the military in solving internal conflicts. The best example is *Brigadier-General Malak Awyen*'s program, which advocates contemporary military supremacy - a typical militarization of the minds of many in South Sudan. Why does the state not show us the same military participating in agricultural projects, building bridges, evacuating people during floods, and preventing inter-communal conflicts since these are the biggest problems facing Jonglei State and many other parts of the country?

State media should be involved in security-related activities that promote the consolidation of efficient, accountable, and professional defense, and the security forces operating under responsible civilian control and supervision. State media should also promote the involvement of civil society organizations as partners in national security and cluster activities. The government should establish effective civilian control over the armed forces and national laws governing the conduct and activities of the armed forces. It's no secret that battlefield trauma can leave veterans with deep emotional scars that affect their ability to function in civilian life[6]. But new research suggests that even without combat, military service has a subtle lasting effect on a man's personality, potentially making it harder for veterans to get along with friends, family, colleagues, and the society at large. It is assumed that all the bad

---

[6] https://source.wustl.edu/2012/02/military-service-changes-personality-makes-vets-less-agreeable/

guys are in the military as they always tend to be more aggressive, more interested in rivalry than teamwork, and less concerned with the feelings of others.

Military personnel are initially a little less cordial and friendly, and military experience seems to confirm this - for, after the war, men perform worse in a military field than men who did not join the military, that is, they determine their ways of handling issues and never follow civilian advice. I went through 45 days of military training in Sudan after I left secondary school in 2010. For me, the military puts you in one of those situations in life where someone else completely controls your daily actions and thinking. It is where from the moment you wake up in the morning until you go to bed at night, someone actively works to break down anything individual about you and while building him or herself. The scaring reality that military men operate under commands and orders of their superiors can prove to be lethal if it interferes in nation-building as things will fall apart, just like the current stagnant status of South Sudan that is wrestling protracted conflicts since independence[7]. Many young people join the military with the sole goal that it will *make them one man* - a kind of thinking used by the militarized political forces to lead the country into destruction, anarchy, and endless wars - for eight years.

The tendency to use violence in resolving political problems is among the key dangers of militaristic modes of governance such as the current R-TGoNU, and out of necessity, peace agreements are negotiated between the warring parties, which gives priority to military leaders. However, the sustainability of such an agreement will much depend on the demilitarization of governance - which means involving unarmed politicians in the governance structures at the national, state, and local levels. This in turn is closely linked to the extent to which different social groups can be involved in a peace settlement. My greatest concern is how to support the most vulnerable groups in our society - women, young people, and the poor, both the poor and the marginalized, who also have the greatest interest in peace - to be heard while having their presence felt and be regarded as a contribution to sustainable peace which we all desire. This is a laudable objective.

---

[7] Wounds of War: How the VA Delivers Health, Healing, and Hope to the Nation's Veterans - Book by Suzanne Gordon

Demilitarizing Our Mindsets

Who in their right minds would even dare to oppose women, young people, and the poor, facilitating peace? There is no doubt that these are the people most exposed to the great burdens and risks during armed conflicts, especially the protracted internal conflicts that are all too common in the various parts of South Sudan. Those who want to organize peace groups or peace movements in South Sudan face enormous challenges. Opportunities for civil society and social mobilization are limited. Moreover, the power relations inherent in armed conflict tend to further subjugate such people and make their participation in the country's political life more problematic. The predominance of militarism is perhaps the only major obstacle to effective social mobilization.

We must also bear in mind that these categories are not without complications. Women, young people, and the poor are not organic social groups that automatically stick together. They pledge multiple loyalties to different groups and especially in wartime because some of these loyalties go to either ethnic groups, religions or political parties. Many young and poor people, and some women, are themselves fighters. It is often overlooked how ordinary soldiers are victims of war, how they suffer the highest casualties, and although some of them inflict physical and mental abuse, they are also direct victims of abuse. Since they have established a military hierarchy at the bottom, they cannot express their views without risking a trial before a court-martial for rebellion or worse. What strategies can be pursued for those who work for these marginalized groups?

We need to identify and associate ourselves with the different types of civil society activities that are related to peace, governance, human rights, and the mobilization of social progress and change. Mobilizing grassroots organizations and individuals en masse to pursue common interests is a commendable broad moral cause. Besides, policy-oriented advocacy is the activism of professionals in the field who can bring the issue to the public, provide legal and policy expertise, while advising governments and international organizations. Investigations must thoroughly be carried out to expose the overwhelming rot within the militarized system of public administration and to bring to justice all culprits while providing legal assistance to the victims. Journalism and law will always be crucial in demilitarizing our war-ravaged nation.

Entrenched *'Gabilia'*

Our liberators fought disunity but we are fighting unity!

Undeniably, colonialism fostered deep-rooted hatred through the divide and rule policy to strengthen the imperialists' political and administrative control, which left devastating trails of hatred among African communities, some of which prevail to date. Since independence in 2011, South Sudan has spent more years at war with itself than in peace while it has never experienced a democratic rule of law. Tribalism *(Gabilia)* is a tool used by politicians in South Sudan to mobilize fellow tribesmen to rally behind them in fulfilling their tribalistic agendas along their ethnic lines. The British colonialists once used this system, followed by the former Sudan regime to divide the South Sudanese along tribal lines and ultimately drawing them into endless inter-tribal armed conflicts. They intended to drive the communities out of their ancestral lands and then occupy them. This perpetual habit developed into cronyism after South Sudan's independence, where incumbent *Uncles* appointed their next of kin to state institutions and affiliated organizations. By asserting these positions within their families, they aim to serve their greedy tribal interests rather than the common interests of the people of the new nation.

It has become so common to find that if the boss in a government parastatal is *Mr. Mading*, then anyone called *Mabior, Mayan, Madiit,* and *M'aker* can automatically qualify for any public position. Similarly, if the boss is *Mr. Gatluak*, then anyone called *Gatwech* and *Tut* can automatically qualify for any position in that parastatal to claim their tribal rights. Furthermore, when *Mr. Wani* is the boss, he will invite *Lado, Jada,* and *Kenyi* for appointments in the department he leads. It does not matter whether the organization is state or church-owned, even if it is a non-governmental organization, they will still invite their tribesmen to fill all the vacant positions. In this way, tribalism compromises our social fabric and harmony, and it can only be healed through appropriate education and change of mentality, whether *Mading, Gatluak,* or *Wani* are in a leadership position or not, so long as they step down at the end of their term of office to transfer leadership to other capable ones, regardless of which tribe they belong to. Both the Executive and the Legislature have deprived traditional chiefs of their former functions and roles within the communities instead of reintegrating them into new roles within the government or offering viable alternatives. This has led to discrepant and disproportionate local governance systems that have contributed to the prevailing perceptions of inequality, including the lack of female participation, which are often assumed to be based on tribalism, regardless of whether they are qualified or not.

Corruption has spawned tribalism in South Sudan, and the government's inability to control it was portrayed in 2012 when *President Salva Kiir* issued a pathetic call to his government officials to return stolen cash. The 2013 *Oyee Party* internal conflict took a tribal stance that illustrated the prevalence of political tribalism at the highest executive office and the protective elitist class in the country. Tribalism has provided a lens through which power struggles have been framed throughout most of South Sudan's recent history that revolves around the militarized politics of the *SPLM/A* party. We are also overtaken by the perceptions of exclusion and marginalization from those in authority, often accompanied by ethnic scapegoating that has caused immense devastation and dismay.

The close link between tribalism, armed conflict, and the struggle for survival became stronger during South Sudan's decades-long civil war, which involved all 64 ethnic groups. This militarization of ethnic identity became apparent after the *SPLM/A* split in 1991 led by *Dr. Riek Machar* and *Dr. Lam Akol* after an opposing resolution used by the *SPLM/A* in 2013 revived old resentments which led to an all-out civil war at the expense of innocent lives. Consequently, armed violence between the two opposing factions has become increasingly tribalistic, leading to indiscriminate attacks on civilians on both sides. Hence, ethnic identities both within and outside the armed forces became clearer, more exclusive, and relevant to the survival of ordinary South Sudanese, with some opting to renounce their identities to save their lives.

Ethnic ties in South Sudan are essential not only for the reliance of civilians on the armed forces and militias on their military commanders and political leaders but also for the assurances of safety and security of that particular tribe. Given the weakness of the formal state outside South Sudan's urban centers, most rural residents understand the need to ensure protection and security as a communal matter, sometimes politicized by incumbent politicians. It is important to note that using ethnicity as a frame of reference in the resurgent armed conflict contrasts with the much more subtle and complex role that communal belonging plays in South Sudan's day-to-day politics. Since the political transition of 2005, the strengthening of political institutions and the state at the local levels of government created a political enterprise in which tribalism has played a central role. Tribalism has become so common that sentiments are cultivated based on loyalty to a tribe and social group.

Our tribes existed long before we were born, we will die and still, they will remain, but it has now become an epidemic, comparable to a viral disease. Tribalists have behaviors, ideologies, and lifestyles that are different from those of other tribes, but what makes them hold each other by the throat are trivial reasons, including an incompatible view of life, disdain for those who differ from them, and foolish expectations that other tribes will bow to them. Others are naturally stubborn and it is their innate culture that compels them to demonstrate their courage, prosperity, political and military power. However, people in every community have their way of thinking and acting, but one person or ethnicity should not grudgingly assert their domination over others.

If there is a person who loots, kills, rapes, and abuses people along tribal lines, then he or she should face every wrath and curse of a crying nation. But nowadays, if you go somewhere where your culture is unfamiliar to the locals, they will demean you based on your appearance or the way you express yourself while making nasty comments criticizing your tribe's traditions and culture as being so backward. Once you make a mistake, they stereotype your tribesmen as being weak, pathetic, lazy, and gullible. I do not know why God created these people, who place the shortcomings of other tribes at the center of their tribal degradation and stereotyping. Why should someone be judged for something to which he or she didn't choose to belong to?

The prevalence of tribalism in South Sudan is beyond our imagination, but warring tribesmen keep piling up negative perceptions about each other. In common parlance, some tribes are best known for committing some of the most heinous acts that this

Entrenched 'Gabilia'

country has witnessed, including looting, rape, land grabbing, conflict crimes, corruption, and the recruitment of tribal colleagues to *executive* positions. Just as tribalism has no public shame, so do those who practice it with great zeal, without fear of consequences, including the brazen appointment of certain tribal members to public offices. In South Sudan, tribal warfare has affected all facets of our daily lives in such a way that we cannot even surmise what we can achieve individually or collectively without riding along with the wave of tribal warfare.

Some incompetent leaders and ruthless youths have worked so diligently to advance their tribal agenda, even imposing it on others, rather than fostering unity and cohesion among the people of South Sudan. But we must expose the ringleaders who encourage these hideous social vices to proliferate, by stopping them from bringing our new nation to eternal doom. Our liberation heroes disappointed us by not working hard to eradicate the tribalism disease among the people of the new nation that they gifted autonomy. Where is that freedom today, and yet the misery from the evils of tribalism in modern South Sudan keeps worsening by the day? Who supplies the young people in the cattle camps with firearms? Exposing the main perpetrators of tribalism and its affiliated conflicts in South Sudan will not only help our country get rid of these vermin but will make all South Sudanese immensely proud of their homeland, as it will encourage them to cooperate in a country of freedom of expression, development, equal opportunities, and respect for human rights.

Stylish But 'Uneducated'

A swanky accoutre won't put food on the table!

If education qualifications were determined by how people dressed up, then without a doubt, the South Sudanese folks would be the world's most educated, based on their funky dressing standards. Whether you are unemployed or already employed, you must look stylish and swanky. In the new nation, we have more students than ever before who are out of school and stagnant with a failed education system that was wrecked by the *SPLM/A* war of 2013. This is a bad sign, given the lack of trained teachers, inadequate teaching materials, and dilapidated learning infrastructure that failed to meet the ever-increasing demands of a 21st-century learning environment. It is for the same reason that our education is not as competitive as that of the other countries in the Eastern Africa region. This has led to the mass exodus of South Sudanese students to flock learning institutions in the neighboring countries.

The prevalence of conflicts has reduced funding allocation for education resulting in a shortage of teachers, dilapidated infrastructure, poorly stocked libraries, and the misuse of learning facilities for military purposes, especially during the *2013 - 2020 SPLM/A* conflict. These conflicts have led to a serious decline in our academic standards and have lowered the morale of our students and teachers, some of whom are recruited by militias. Even those already at school are not benefiting much from the substandard education which makes them no different from the other children who opt to miss school and romp around the city streets or who wrestle with their cows in the cattle camps. Therefore, the country's education sector is akin to a bed-ridden patient on a drip in the hospital.

Nevertheless, the ubiquity of private institutions in our education system is increasingly being recognized and acknowledged, but still cannot fill the gaps left by the demise of some public institutions. The rise of private schools should not be perceived in a negative light but as a viable alternative to a failing public education system that produces half-baked graduates. According to the World Bank, the high quality of a country's education is a strong indicator of economic growth as nations benefit from a well-educated populace that possesses competent skills and knowledge to advance the key economic sectors such as oil, agriculture, mining, regional and international organizations. Before Sudan's independence in 1956, the British colonial administration had very little educational infrastructure established in southern Sudan, however, Christian missionaries assumed responsibility for formal education but only taught about serving God with tithe and offerings.

Education in southern Sudan suffered immensely during Sudan's subsequent civil wars *(1955–72, 1983–2005)* as national authorities curtailed missionary activities, attempted to Arabize the southern schools, and when they failed, they then closed them in 1962. Beginning in the late 1980s, the *United Nations Children's Fund (UNICEF)* coordinated educational reforms and reconstruction efforts in southern Sudan, but limited resources continued to be a stumbling block, as was the ongoing civil conflict which plunged our education system into an abyss for the last 50 years. For the same period, people in southern Sudan were deprived of the opportunity to enjoy their universal rights to basic education. Even after South Sudan gained independence in 2011 which ended the war and amid efforts to improve educational opportunities in the country, only about half of the children in the school-going age have access to the already-fragile education. For school-going girls, access is even almost non-existent as the majority drop out of school within the first few years due to cultural pressures such as the common tendency of being married off at a young age.

Besides, the educational system is further constrained by the lack of school buildings and in some schools by the risky and dilapidated buildings, the inadequate furniture, the limited number of qualified teachers, and the lack of government incentives to improve learning, especially in rural schools. The civil war of 2013 further devastated the fragile education system, leading to a total standstill of all learning across the country. The fact that South Sudan, ravaged by decades of civil war, has long been deprived of an adequate education system is evident in its literacy rates which are the lowest in the Eastern Africa region. Only about a quarter of South Sudanese adults can read, and due to the gap in literacy rates between men and women, just about two-fifths of men can read and write, while about one-sixth of women can read and write. There are 64 different ethnic groups in South Sudan, each with a long history of customs and traditions. Nevertheless, the Sudanese government made a decades-long attempt to forcibly Arabize the southern region, denying South Sudanese people basic access to education that meets international standards. Despite all, we still cherish our rich cultural diversity that deserves to be taught to our children in primary school - this has an essence of diversity, acceptance, and rejuvenation of our heritage.

Many adults missed school because of war and displacement resulting in the breakdown of the education system, and now we spend less than 2% of our GDP on education, but our children should never suffer the same fate. The lack of access to basic education and training is probably one of the main causes of several other social ills, including the relentless unrest, but we must address this by taking a step back in the chain of causes and effects, to promote and raise awareness of the importance of education in any progressive-minded society. Almost all young people, especially girls, do not know what formal education is all about which is why their parents believe that going to school is a waste of time and that they should be married off instead. All the time, I meet sorrowful university graduates who regret having gone to school because they have failed to find any employment opportunities, and more so, they do not have connections to the pot-bellied *Uncles* who can connect them to suitable job opportunities both in the private and public sectors. Education is important for South Sudan, but the imparting of cultural knowledge is considered the most essential by all the 64 ethnic groups.

In the past, even today, an older child was not, and still is not, allowed to go to school because of the cultural beliefs attached to them such as being the heir to the family estate, and as a future head of the family. Without a doubt, if my father had stayed in the village where such beliefs abound and persist, I would have been one of the armed illiterates and warriors who foolishly attack other communities during cattle raids. Perhaps I would have been killed or injured in some of the communal conflicts, as the majority of my peers were killed, while others were wounded or coerced into joining the military. As for formal progressive education, our cultural beliefs and the tribes' warped attitude to literacy are detrimental to raising a self-sustaining nation of hardworking, intelligent, and enlightened workforce. We should resolve to put an end to distorted cultural perceptions about formal education and advocate on behalf of every South Sudanese to gain relevant education irrespective of family status, gender, or cultural affiliations.

Over the next decade, a massive modernization of school infrastructure to meet global learning standards is needed to improve our education sector. Only a competent government can recognize the need to invest immensely in the education of its citizens to produce highly skilled technocrats to manage our natural resources competently and responsibly. The case of South Sudan is unique given the high illiteracy rate that we should solve by training our children in practical skills through *Technical Vocational Education and Training (TVET)*. In other countries, *TVETs* have encouraged the acquisition and development of entrepreneurial and innovative skills for self-employment. Most Chinese working in South Sudan are not university graduates, but well-equipped technicians or *TVET* graduates.

If the government is serious about empowering the youth, it should strategically build *TVET* colleges in each state, equip them with modern learning facilities, equipment, and qualified training staff. We also need to promote early childhood education to lay firm foundations for our children's' stabilized socio-emotional development. More often, early childhood education facilitates our young ones to choose suitable career paths, starting with identifying their unique talents followed by proper guidance to ensure their success in school, obtain a decent job, and income - all along while positively influencing others. Although as adults we missed this crucial stage in our lives, we should make sure that our children do not miss it as well.

Investing in early childhood development can greatly benefit the younger generation in South Sudan and the communities from which they come which can help to close the gap in early childhood development between South Sudan and other countries in the region. Children who participate in preschool programs are more likely to come from affluent households, though children in low-income communities across the country would also benefit most from such programs if they were extended closer to them wherever they are, whether in slums or villages. Preschool programs should aim at preparing young children for a good start in their school career. Millions of infants under the age of five are not reaching their full life development potential due to the absence of early childhood education programs. As governments focus on providing better educational opportunities for school-age children, preschool classes must be taken into account. Access to high-quality pre-primary education can improve a child's primary education outcomes and life chances.

Several African nations took an important step in the right direction by abolishing tuition fees to allow more children to attend primary school. The outcome was promising, but maintaining high-quality primary education remains a huge challenge for most countries, especially in young South Sudan. In the new nation, we should also consider abolishing tuition fees for primary education from the first to the sixth grade, just like how Uganda introduced *Universal Primary and Secondary Education (Education for all)*. State-supported academic programs are also needed through the provision of scholarships to needy but bright students, in addition to improving access to student loans for working students in higher education institutions. Eliminating tuition fees, investing in education infrastructure and resources, and school lunches will surely help to boost enrollment by millions.

Secondary education is crucial to preparing students for higher education and important life skills as it provides the skills and tools necessary for meeting the country's growing demands for highly skilled and educated workers in a globalized world. African governments are increasingly recognizing the need to invest in and expand access to secondary education, and so should South Sudan. Our government should ensure high-quality upper secondary education to prepare students for universities and *TVETs* to facilitate them in producing high-quality graduates with the much-needed skills for the local labor market. Today, secondary education is still predominantly reserved for the privileged few, however, the government's task is to ensure an all-inclusive education that benefits all regardless of affordability. So we must not only expand secondary education, but also improve the quality of education and its output. Developing and nurturing the technical and professional skills helps to diversify our people's employment opportunities in the local market. Skilled workers also create an attractive economic environment for investors.

Challenges to education in South Sudan

When it comes to issues of education quality and equity, there are underlying causes that prevent progress, such as the frequency of conflicts that led to high dropout rates, class repetition, poor quality of education and academic resources, teacher shortages, poor infrastructure and supplies, inaccessibility to education for rural and remote areas, and the stigmatization of marginalized groups. In the next decade, more than ten thousand youths are expected to join South Sudan's labor market yearly. Job creation in the country is largely within the informal economy, which absorbs even those who cannot find work in the formal sector. Due to the sky-rocketing unemployment rates and the prevalence of nepotism in the job market, graduates with secondary and tertiary education are now into self-employment as they launch *small and medium-sized enterprises (SMEs)* instead of opting for white-collar employment. This is a positive sign that needs our collective support as it sends a strong message that young people are tired of wandering the dusty streets of the city searching for an *Uncle* in the government who will help them find a job.

While *TVETs* foster a skilled workforce, such training does not create jobs unless government incentives are provided. If our children lack adequate work and life skills, many will face an uncertain future. Governments and the private sector alike must develop labor-development and training programs that recognize the need for young people to be self-employed or work for small businesses. As the world becomes more technologically advanced, South Sudan's school curricula must evolve to provide the appropriate education and training for today's technical workforce. There remains a serious mismatch between the skills possessed by the young South Sudanese workers and the skills employers critically need, with most students graduating from neighboring countries including Uganda, Kenya, Ethiopia, and Sudan. The government must look into helping private schools pay their teaching and non-teaching staff to ensure an uninterrupted learning environment.

Where possible, teacher training colleges need to be established across the country to properly train, instruct, and produce highly-qualified teachers. By posting competent teachers to rural schools with attractive incentives, the government will greatly improve the country's education standards without leaving any tribe, region, and state behind. Since rural teachers are less qualified than their urban counterparts, more needs to be done to support teacher training in the rural areas because, in one instance, teachers were made to sit for the same test as their students, and three-quarters of them failed.

Besides, students who do not receive the same education as those in urban areas will always have difficulty reading, writing, and calculating simple mathematical tasks, even after graduation. Nor do such students achieve the same results during their careers. Since education is a crucial element in building stabilized career paths, the South Sudanese government must be aware that equal access to basic and formal education needs to be guaranteed in all regions and states of the country. We want our government to focus on upgrading its education systems to match international standards and the employers' expectations. This will in turn guarantee our country a sufficient human capital base that can respond and meet the ever-changing needs of a developing nation.

To increase literacy rates, education should be the government's top priority, with 20% of the national budget earmarked for improving the education system. Since the conflict outbreak in 2013, military expenditure has sabotaged funding for other key sectors such as health, agriculture, public service, and education. Awkwardly, South Sudan is among the 21 African countries identified globally as the biggest spenders of their GDP on defense and security in comparison to the amount of money spent in the education sector. As South Sudanese, there is nothing that can give us immense joy and pride other than belonging to a forward-marching and developed South Sudan, but that is only possible once we prioritize education that not only transforms the individual but also revolutionizes South Sudan into a very powerful and regionally influential country.

Silencing the Guns

Can't we just give peace a chance to flourish?

Wars in South Sudan are always silly games orchestrated by foes harboring political and tribal resentments against each other. As they can't fight by themselves, they entice young people with no military experience to fight and murder on their behalf because war is their bread for survival. It has become so easy to lure the desperate unemployed young people with false promises of money and jobs in return for them risking their lives. In just seven years of civil war, thousands of young people lost their lives at the hands of their reckless leaders, who were once considered liberators. The conflicts that led to the downfall of the *SPLM/A* house quickly escalated to devastate the whole nation, forcing people to become refugees in their own country in the *United Nations Protection of Civilians (POC)* sites, while others crossed over to neighboring countries for asylum and peaceful sanctuary. The 2013 conflict was by no means a noble thing. It was an appalling tragedy, and its aftermath is part of the dark years of our history, a state of anarchy that it was. Yet, the people of South Sudan once fought noble liberation wars against the Khartoum-based Sudanese regime. These guerilla wars included the First Sudanese Civil War *(1955-1972)* and the Second Sudanese Civil War *(1983-2005)*.

Different communities collectively and voluntarily sent their sons and daughters to war zones with the sole aim of liberating their ancestor's lands from the dictatorial Khartoum regime which denied us our right to participate in the nation's building and development. The people of South Sudan have contributed not only human resources to the liberation movements but also their livestock, including cows, goats, and sheep, to the brave soldiers on the front line. They gave willingly and wholeheartedly because they valued peace above all else and insisted on achieving it at all costs. During the war, when I was a little boy, I remember my mother asking me to look out for the arrival of military combatants on our premises. As soon as I saw armored vehicles, I hurried off to alert my mother about the approaching army. She would immediately split our food in half, voluntarily giving one half of our food to the military and keeping the other half in a hidden place so that we could remain with something to eat. One day they came unexpectedly and took all our food, and we had to starve.

In 2005, the *Comprehensive Peace Agreement (CPA)* was signed by two rival parties - the *SPLM/A* and the Sudanese government to end the longest civil war on the African continent, which claimed the lives of two million people. Moreover, the *CPA* granted the Southern Sudanese people the right of self-determination through independence from the former Sudan republic. At least 98% of South Sudanese voted unanimously for secession and earned their independence on 9 July 2011. The independence of the South Sudanese people was associated with great expectations that their new country and government would live up to their expectations and wishes with hopes that peace and socio-economic transformation would become prioritized. Unfortunately, in 2013, the land of great abundance once again plunged into a seven-year civil war triggered by turmoil within the ruling party, the *SPLM/A*, and issues regarding internal elections rules after *President Salva Kiir* was appointed party leader in 2008.

Leadership interests emerged within the party as loyal cadres like *Dr. Riek Machar (the then Vice President of South Sudan and Deputy Chair of SPLM), Pagan Amum (the then SPLM secretary-general), Mama Nyandeng Garang De Mabior (a member of SPLM political bureau)*, and others expressed interest in leading the party. Dust was raised and things started falling apart as the ruling party disintegrated into two rival factions: *the SPLM/A In-Charge*, and *the SPLM/A-In-Opposition*. Former prisoners, as well as the disgruntled members and other smaller discontented cliques, re-emerged with opposing agendas, all of which exposed the utter chaos, obscurity, and political dilemma that brought the whole country to a complete standstill. This senseless war by the *SPLM/A* elites has not only deprived our communities of the social and economic development they truly deserve but has also robbed them of their constitutional right to safety, justice, and security. From just internal party wrangles, the country slipped into a state of anarchy, where anyone in combat gear and carrying a gun took the law in their hands without anyone stopping them. The war has thrown South Sudanese communities into disarray, with criminals and outlaws taking advantage of the chaos to plunder, kill and enrich themselves at the expense of the nation's peace and development.

Now that peace is gradually returning to the nation, there is no reason why these debilitated parties cannot push ahead with the implementation of the revived peace agreement so that the people of South Sudan can enjoy the peace to restore their cohesion and harmony. War is destructive and traumatizing, it destroys lives, and the victims have been psychologically scarred for decades, which explains why all - young and old - should do everything to engage conflict resolution measures instead of causing violence. Despite the pariah status of our country, there is still a huge potential for investment and improvement in the general human development index, but only if we pursue peace first. War is unpleasant, and we should avoid it at all costs. In all these years I have fought for peace instead of violence, and I have never repaid hatred with hatred, but with peace, love, justice, and tranquility. Where there is peace, weapons are of no use, for people will be walking in the same direction, agreeing on issues, and compromising.

Inter-ethnic wars

The South Sudanese who are still viciously killing themselves in bloody ethnic fighting and those who are dying in these senseless conflicts are all young men and women whose services are urgently needed to reconstruct the new nation of South Sudan. The horrific inter-community attacks only leave us wondering why certain tribesmen can simply attack and kill at will anyone different from them, kidnap children, rape women, burn their homes and gardens in broad daylight with impunity, steal cattle, all under the watchful eye of the authorities. Some reports put death figures in the first quarter of 2020 alone at 658, while 592 women and children were abducted and 65 cases of sexual abuse were documented among the young people during that period. The paramount question is: what causes these inter-ethnic wars between our communities and how do we resolve them? Even among the tea ladies at the Konyokonyo market, it is a known belief that these conflicts are caused by cattle rustling, land disputes, kidnappings of children, raping of defenseless women, traditional forced marriages, and intertribal land conflicts.

But one reason that has been overlooked time and again in the discussion of this issue is the proliferation of firearms in the hands of the civilian population. This one hidden reason will later prove to be a decisive factor in creating an enabling environment for inter-ethnic wars and insecurity between our communities. There is also a common sense of understanding and agreement that this said factor causes the continuous inter-ethnic conflicts among communities in Jonglei, Unity, Upper Nile, and the Lakes States. The president has, on this basis, issued many decrees for civilians to peacefully or voluntarily surrender their weapons to the state. But the answer has always been: *"I bought this weapon from Russia in exchange for my cow."* The president's order became a futile attempt at reducing ethnic armed violence by making communities weapons-free. Unfortunately, the decades of civil war, the arming of our civilian population by proxies serving government and rebel groups, and the ill-disciplined SSPDF have contributed negatively to the ongoing communal conflicts. To this day, interethnic wars and uncertainties continue to engulf every part of South Sudan.

Therefore, the formation of recurring conflict committees and televised presidential decrees are frivolous and cannot go deep into resolving the problem of communal conflicts, led by the uninformed young people. This problem not only kills our public morale but also causes mental disorders in our people and obscures the peaceful and nonviolent aspirations of our communities. Indeed, it is a miserable thing for the young men and women to succumb to a culture of mutual killing and revenge. We were not born on this earth to do deadly battles as our business, and so it is a depressing thing to bear which we must end now before we live to regret it for the remainder of our lives. The prevalent gun culture in our societies not only fosters communal conflicts but also harbors criminal practices including land grabbing, daytime and night robberies, rape, murder, to name but a few. As civilians have easy access to firearms, these proliferating crimes highlight the fact that the lack of arms control or disarmament of civilians is detrimental to our social stability and security.

It is therefore necessary that our leaders develop strategies to curb the growing possession of weapons by our civilian population. We all know that in some parts of our societies, weapons are sold to civilians or traded in exchange for cows - particularly in the Upper Nile, Jonglei, and Bahr el Ghazal. In that case, it will be difficult for a civilian to hand over weapons to the authorities without being compensated in cash or with a cow, thus creating the compensation factor that is most appropriate for disarmament. Gun control is therefore akin to trying to regulate drivers who drink alcohol to reduce car crashes on the roads. The use of firearms is intended to protect the territory of the country and its people, but it is disheartening that most of my peers, who were born in the 1990s, have lost their lives in such terrible tribal conflicts, which has deprived us the young people of the hope for the development of our society with which we would have immensely contributed positively to the development of South Sudan.

Historically, our communities have long been engaged in inter-ethnic and inter-communal violence. Instead of learning how to live together peacefully, we decided to collide with each other and sow the seeds of hatred among their children to pass on the hate. There must be laws restricting civilian access to weapons to curb gun violence and reduce the number of gun crimes and deaths within communities. There is a need for political leaders to actively engage the conflicting communities and address their grievances to resolve the various community problems they face. The role of NGOs, communities, and religious organizations in creating public awareness regarding the prevention of tribal violence should never be underestimated because they are the ones operating at the grassroots level within these communities, and therefore understand the situation much better. It is also important that intellectuals take the lead in assisting local leaders to solve problems and raising awareness to be informed about the right decisions such as advocating for the sending of children to school who will later improve their families, communities, and country in the future.

For much of its existence, South Sudan was never at peace with itself as civil violence began long before independence in 2011. The 2010 general elections, which led to popular discontent across the country, had the immediate effect of creating rebel movements that were composed of disgruntled refugees financed by the Khartoum regime. Moreover, before the 2010 elections, there was a well-known predominant policy of the *SPLM/A* to bring all South Sudanese on board and ensure a successful independence referendum which later took place in 2011. After independence and under the *SPLM/A* regime, many militias with higher military ranks were absorbed into the national liberation army. These absorbed militias ultimately grew in ranks and outnumbered the liberation army with promotions to the ranks of Officer Corp. But the unintended effect of this initiative was its ability to incentivize rebellion, making it difficult for South Sudanese to build a stable and prosperous country. To create an inclusive South Sudan and portray it as a land governed by the rule of law, the militia groups must be disbanded, tribalism eradicated instead of being rewarded as is the current norm. Penalizing rebellion and rewarding state loyalty would work to create a more promising political culture and stability which can also inspire virtuous and patriotic citizens.

While South Sudan was fighting to gain its independence from Sudan, hundreds of women and men sacrificed their precious lives and shed blood so that the new nation could rise strongly from the ashes. Their spilled blood should never be in vain, unlike now, when selfish opportunists are seeking to destroy the liberators' hard-earned legacy. Our liberators died with confidence that South Sudan will finally be free and that there will be no more bloodshed. With all that is going on, I believe they are turning in their graves because of the shameful and despicable behaviors of the current leaders. Some of them, I guess could be wishing that they had not died because what is being done now is the total opposite of what they believed in while fighting for our liberty. But what do the dead know? They do not know what the people they fought for are going through today, perhaps if there is anything they were so sure of before they were finally lowered into their graves, it was the freedom they finally brought their people. They were sure that their children and the widows they left behind would reap the fruits of their struggle, but this never happened.

To this day, innocent people are still losing their lives recklessly while the perpetrators forget that these are their fellow countrymen and women whom they keep pursuing as sworn enemies. Communities that once lived side by side were divided along ethnic lines; even those that once shared communal land are now foes because of political divisions. While foreigners are busy capitalizing on the country's resources to gain unprecedented wealth, citizens are tearing each other apart, as no one seems to care. The foreigners came here nine years ago and have earned billions of dollars in profits which they repatriate to their home countries, and the South Sudanese are still impoverished, with only Russian AK47s in their possession.

Guns were used during the liberation struggle for South Sudan's freedom, and when that mission was accomplished, these weapons had to be put back in the armories so that peace can prevail and people work together for the betterment of the country. But unfortunately, it seems that our people cannot live without guns which is worrisome.

Deceitful Political Dreams

After a decade since independence, many common folks are still losing their precious lives daily. No decent schools, no proper roads, and the health system remain in tatters. The future of the country hangs in balance because apart from destruction and displacement there is absolutely nothing to be proud of when we scrutinize ourselves. All we care about is competition for brand new weapons to brag about, rather than productively thinking about developing ourselves and our country.

We are no longer in control of our key sectors because foreign businessmen outsmarted us and are running them, but we can not keep trusting them to have the patriotic spirit to develop South Sudan, so it is shameful that we have abandoned our prized resources to them, including price regulation. When you look at some of these gun-toting lads, most of them are young people who should be in school learning how to contribute to the country's development. The future of the country is in the hands of the young people who must never accept involvement in the politics of killing one another for monetary and political gains. But, faced with these murders, one may even be tempted to wonder how it would be possible to envisage a better South Sudan in the subsequent ten years, just as we were about to celebrate our tenth anniversary and then things became worse. How can that be possible in chaotic situations? Well, a better South Sudan will never be achieved if we continue these tribal wars, which is why we need our young guys to join us to set a fine example for others in nation-building. Young people must be the ones to preach peace and, on top of that, come together as a family with a strong interest in moving South Sudan forward. We should also demand our legitimate representation in governance structures at all national levels and down to the Boma level. The young people must be given seats at the national table, or else they will create their own.

Strategies for Silencing the Guns

Our dreams of a conflict-free South Sudan will only come true in the absence of wars, inter-ethnic conflicts, gender-based violence, and genocide in the country. Abolishing illicit gun trade is a key component in eliminating all forms of gun-related violence. Illegal gun trade in Africa accounts for roughly $2 billion or nearly 20% of the global arms trade. In South Sudan, the arms trade is becoming the new normal, as global corporations participate in lucrative arms sales for profits. Widespread misuse of weapons diverts scarce government resources leading to instability which drags investment and economic growth. We must recognize that the production and trade of weapons of war is largely a legal endeavor - the problem is when these weapons are diverted to the illegal market, where the use of small arms becomes the country's distinct feature.

Another common feature is the impracticality of development in South Sudan: conflicts that escalated with the availability of weapons undermined the quest for peace and security that became the greatest challenge facing the new nation. Silencing the guns is not simply the government's responsibility alone, but also the duty of every peace-loving individual, coupled with the participation of other strategic actors and institutions who should send out a strong united voice to the foreigners profiting from the lucrative arms deals within the country. The voice of the South Sudanese is one, loud, and clear: We do not need the proliferation of arms and weapons in the new nation. The outbreak of violence in 2013 showed a huge deficit in the government's professionalization of the military, the failure to manage the diversity of our population, and poor governance. A lasting solution is to address these important factors that lead to violence and conflict throughout the country.

The participation of women in peace efforts is another important step that should be taken seriously to integrate them into all government structures and to recruit them into the armed forces to reduce gender violence and inequality in the country's security structures. The early warning mechanism is an idea that focuses on early conflict detection, prevention, and swift response. The 2013 conflict was predicted in March of the same year because almost all South Sudanese knew that the *SPLM/A* would at any time be embroiled in a violent confrontation within the foreseeable future. Time and again, the possibility of violence was discussed in the media and tea rooms, and the civil war broke out nine months later in December. As usual, the army rallied behind its tribalistic leaders. Early prevention could have prevented this civil war as early as May 2013, when the signs became clear after President Kiir dissolved the entire cabinet in one night, with 75 cabinet ministers sent home on the president's orders. Likewise, conflicts can be predicted from political build-ups that may become tense overnight and later spreading into national turmoils.

Therefore, to silence the guns in South Sudan, we must begin at the family level to teach our children the need for peaceful coexistence and to educate them about coexistence with people from cultures other than their own. While it is difficult to find parents who previously experienced violence and now advocate for peace at the family level, it remains a prerequisite for nurturing a culture of harmony and conciliation at home. It is therefore necessary to include adult education that teaches about peacebuilding and peacekeeping. For peace to be adopted as a culture in South Sudan, it is necessary to coordinate grassroots efforts where children can learn about forgiveness, rapprochement, and coexistence.

Primary school textbooks should be modified to meet our expectations of a peaceful country where peaceful means of conflict resolution is at the heart of our education system. Noteworthy examples include *Gatluak, Deng,* and *Wani,* who reconciled to advance a common prospect under a unified vision of harmony. Asserting our social values should be by involving citizens in strengthening our national unity to bring greater stability and social cohesion in the long term. In addition to the *UNMISS,* there is an urgent need to step up diplomatic efforts to stabilize the country after a long period of conflict. Establishment of the *National Early Warning System (NEWS),* which, through various early warning tools and the culture of national mediation, with some external support or even without outside interference, can prevent conflicts from taking place. We also need the involvement of our wise elders and others with a repute for advocating for peaceful means of ending disagreements to voluntarily act as the supreme office for the prevention of violence, followed by the swift action of the institutions working on peace initiatives and implementation.

Civil society, the private sector, human rights organizations, faith groups, and other development partners can serve as watchdogs for the *National Early Warning Mechanism (NEWM)* in reporting timely warnings of violence and conflict so that preventive strategies can be applied. Predictable conflicts, such as the *SPLM/A*'s 2013 house collapse, can be avoided if we implement all the mechanisms discussed across the country, especially in major cities. *Disarmament, Demobilization, and Reintegration (DDR)* is another central component in silencing the guns of violence in the new nation. *DDR* is when the most vulnerable combatants are disarmed and screened out, such as the children and the elderly in the armed forces. This process helps to professionalize the military so that it fits the standards of a National Army that protects state interests. The national army should be diversified and made gender-equal, while being open to recruits from all the 64 ethnic groups to avoid nurturing tribalism within the army, especially when most recruits come from either the Dinka, Nuer, and or Choluok tribes. The increased presence of women in the military will reduce gender bias, rape, and other forms of sexual degradation or exploitation by the ill-disciplined military men who are but a group of tribal fighters.

The men and women in the national army and other security agencies should receive their salaries in time to deter them from harassing citizens for money and other valuables. Back to my point, the failure to prevent civilians from accessing guns became a catalyst for conflicts after the formation of a transitional government in 2016. The detection and prevention of conflicts can be implemented immediately after the signing of the peace agreement, and the ceasefire is only one part of the overall picture of conflict prevention. Our peacetime youth can focus more on preventive and post-conflict strategies, in which we voluntarily become the champions of peacebuilding, peacemaking, and peacekeeping. The *RTGoNU* can focus on strategies like conflict prevention, crisis management, *Post – Conflict Reconstruction and Development (PCRD)*, addressing strategic security issues, coordination, and partnerships. These may be the ambitions of the current transitional government to put the country on the right track, but the strategies must be adapted and ultimately implemented before it is too late. The long-term transformation of the new nation is a responsibility that rests on the shoulders of both the current and succeeding generations, but it is necessary to foster perseverance and determination to achieve the kind of South Sudan that we all want.

We should develop a holistic effort to silence our guns as a necessity for peace and the only way to realize South Sudan's full potential to transform the lives of all our citizens and future generations to live in sustainable peace, security, and prosperity. It is too easy for political leaders to commit egregious crimes under the law, including the crime of aggression and not to pay the price for the thousands of innocent South Sudanese who disappeared under their watch. Now is the time to change the rules such that those who wage wars have befitting consequences including jail sentences.

Let's end the double standards, and replace might with right through the equitable application of the law. It is time to demand that our leaders explore peaceful ways of resolving conflicts. My thoughts in ending the myriad political wars in South Sudan, especially involving the youth, are that leaders who promote war-like tendencies should be prevented from mobilizing the young people. Otherwise, they should carry their weapons and fight for themselves, but I doubt if they will attempt to.

The collective civil society must expose the muted suffering of our children and the pain they face after the loss of their parents, yet the children of the warmongers are safely abroad. Why should it be that only the children of the poor suffer most? If they want to advance their selfish interests, they must bring their children back to the country and coerce them to wage their fathers' wars and protect their political or military thrones. The civilians should support the established courts of law so that all perpetrators are charged and tried for all egregious war crimes to make them own up the mess and destruction they caused to the country.

In a fully functioning democracy, it is the responsibility of the citizens to exercise control over their leaders who are bent on committing crimes by shamelessly abusing the laws of South Sudan. Impeachment of such leaders can also send a strong message that incompetent leaders cannot be tolerated in any democratic society. Given that the country does not have a permanent constitution, people should wait for it to be promulgated, so that an incumbent president abides by it rather than behaving like an emperor of his village. Citizens should never be tempted to elect officials so militarized that their investment in weapons overshadows our collective vision of a prosperous country. Leaders should also strengthen national mechanisms for post-conflict reconstruction, reintegration, and social development. We say NO to political assassinations, ethnic divisions, and economic marginalization in South Sudan because we are committed to preventing conflict and substituting it with mediation, peace, prosperity, and socio-economic development. LET US RESOLVE TO SILENCE THE GUNS, ONCE AND FOR ALL.

Deceitful Political Dreams

Mischievous bureaucratism is the norm!

Politics is a dirty game of the rich class playing with the rights of the poor, as said by *Ahsan Fareed*. No matter how dirty politics has become, almost all South Sudanese youth want to get involved in politics in one way or another. For a decade and a half, South Sudan's main problem has been poor management by bureaucrats with incompetent leadership which has stalled the country under the incompetent leadership of powerful militarized politicians and *'liberation heroes'*. Bureaucrats are people in a position of authority, such as the President, Minister, Governor, or other government officials, who take no personal financial risks because of their entitlement. They often use a phrase in Arabic to assert their entitlement *'Hakuna Betaana'* implying *Our government*.

Normally bureaucrats are unelected government officials who run a government based on bureaucratic processes. According to the *Oxford English Dictionary*, bureaucratic processes refer to a system of government in which appointed government officials make the most important decisions, not elected officials. Bureaucrats can lose public resources and mismanage them, but they do not lose personal money and instead, they are reshuffled to another public position. They are always highly paid, whether they qualify to occupy a particular office or not. If you look at the bureaucrats who govern South Sudan today, especially our political leaders, I believe most of them condone corruption, although not all in some cases.

Politicians use deceit and cunning, or even criminal behavior, to create political ideologies that would come to nothing without a transformative development agenda that can benefit the country and its growing young population. The big question is why do young people prefer to join the divisive politics rather than emulating our liberation fighters who made significant contributions to South Sudan's independence. Young people are taking the easiest steps to achieve self-fulfillment through a desperate political avenue of greed. But the upright self-realization should be achieved through steps, as highlighted in Abraham Maslow's Hierarchy of Needs he presented in 1943 titled *A Theory of Human Motivation*. Maslow's Hierarchy of Needs suggests that people are motivated to first fulfill their basic needs before moving on to other secondary or more advanced needs, and for sure this cannot be achieved through politics in most cases unless you misappropriate public resources. This hierarchy is presented as a pyramid whereby the bottom levels indicate the basic needs such as food, clothing, and shelter, whereas the more complex needs are at the top and one of these is self-realization, a twisted dream of self-enrichment.

Politicians are always seeking higher positions that give them access to more resources and willpower. In our case, the Boma Administrator aspires to be the Payam Boss, while the Payam Boss is eying for the County Commissioner's post who is also vying for the Governor's position. The same trend is also prevalent at the national level where a Deputy Minister wants the position of his superior and a Minister is someday hoping to occupy the country's topmost office - the Presidency. This is also portrayed in having five Vice Presidents as per the *R-TGoNU* formed in 2020 which assured positions for all the warring 2013 parties. Serving the people at the grassroots level is a redline for many current politicians in South Sudan. The question is if we all aspire to become presidents, then who will work at the grassroots to uplift our people out of poverty and hunger. As young people, we can become the custodians of our respective communities because current leaders have failed to provide access to basic health care, adequate roads, markets for our agricultural products, and to resolve community conflicts, which are often politicized for political gain. We are willing to work with a few leaders who treasure a peaceful, war-free South Sudan, where intergenerational dialogue between the old and the young is at the forefront.

From my perspective, politicians are failing to meet the needs of citizens at Maslow's first and second levels, namely food, health, education, security, peace, and clean water. That is why so many South Sudanese are not satisfied with how the country is administered at all levels because there is no single inclusive plan or strategy to improve our livelihoods and eradicate poverty. Citizens can never feel safe and secure or exercise control over their resources, family security, health, and community property. As the youth of the new nation who play a critical role in shaping sustainable development, we should consider pursuing humane development, unlike our current leaders, who do not care about our welfare and well-being. If politicians are only interested in fattening their potato bellies, the nation's children suffer greatly, and consequently, they flood our streets and turn to crime and violence as their new way of life. Some of them join street crime gangs known as *Awalad Toronto* or *Toronto Boys* living a thug life by robbing people of their valuables and getting away on their *Sanke* Motorcycles. Recently, the *Awalad Toronto* crime gang started robbing Juba women of their much-prized Brazilian Human Hair and wigs on the streets which further shows how dire the situation has become. This is South Sudan that none of us ever dreamed of, and that is why we are calling for a crime-free country and the unmasking of the unknown gunmen. A lot of young people are working for a lasting solution, talking about new ways of self-employment while urging the government to create more jobs for the unemployed, be it an industrial park or modernizing agriculture. I hate critics, but facts must be presented to pave the way for a generation that takes into account and endorses development agendas while leaving room for innovation and creativity.

I know how difficult it is for the young people in this country to make the best use of their *youth vitality*, but it is necessary to embrace the values of morality, creativity, spontaneity, and acceptance of the fact that it is us who are building the country that we all voted for in 2011. We are considered the youngest nation regionally, as 72% of the population is between 15 and 35 years old. Little has been done to achieve the purposeful participation of the youth in governance and sustainable development, and yet they have suffered most from the pervasive internal conflicts and instability since 2013. Recent continental trends have repackaged the concept of *dialogue* into *intergenerational dialogue* to address the gap between the younger and older generations in leadership. I saw it as a dialogue that fosters cooperation between the more conservative older generation and the more liberal younger generation which is the majority and is the most drawn to intergenerational hostilities.

According to the *Mo Ibrahim Index*, the average age of African leaders is 66, while the average age of the continent's population is 25, a staggering 44 years age difference. In South Sudan, the folks in the generation that fought for our independence are the ones warming the leadership seats across all levels of administration in the country. Just check those who sit on national committees for conflicts, disasters and crisis management, economic revitalization, COVID-19 response, and the like, they are all pot-bellied *Uncles*. While the youths are busy arguing over who is the best player between *Ronaldo* and *Messi* at tea places, the pot-bellied old politicians are busy mismanaging our country's affairs the way they want. It is quite obvious that young people are often intimidated by the older generation, while the older generation is afraid to admit that they too are intimidated by the more conscious younger generation. For example, it is difficult for me to have an honest and fruitful one-on-one discussion with my uncle without involving words like *respectful, less knowledgeable, just accept it as it is,* and *"I know everything uncle".* With all due respect, this cultural perspective transcends the boundaries of households to communities and then governance spheres, it has always been the elders to make decisions on our behalf. In today's world, there is an urgent need to break down such politically and militarily motivated barriers that have caused intimidation and fear.

Now it is up to us to find out if the nation owes us anything. If young people ask themselves thought-provoking questions like *What can I do for my country?* then we can be moved to think beyond entitlement attitudes that strip the young citizens of their share of the national cake. If I have the authority, I can introduce compulsory employment for all youth who decide to sit under the trees enjoying uncountable cups of tea, one after another without thinking of finding something productive to do. Brother, just get your ass up and do anything that can keep you busy while contributing to national development, instead of staging political sideshows that take our beloved nation nowhere. The Uncles in public offices also have a role to play in teaching the young people to detach their minds from the *Hakuna betaana* entitlement mentality and teach them how to fish for themselves and assume competent leadership that our country truly deserves.

Young people should stop playing political escapades while dreaming of having huge mansions in Nairobi, Kampala, or the in the western world while staying in hotel rooms in their own country and then expecting to serve the public in a government position. Such lifestyles as copied from our thick-bellied *Uncles* in government should be prevented because we need exemplary leadership that puts humanity above anything else so that every citizen can enjoy a sense of community and national belonging regardless of their ethnic diversity. The idiom *Keeping up with the Joneses* which refers to comparisons with others as a measure of social class or the accumulation of material goods should be kicked out of South Sudan. The *keeping up with the political Joneses* phrase in this book describes the socio-economic status of a government official who loots public resources to live large, buying new *V8 Land Cruisers* whose value is between $80,000 – $100,000. Only one *V8 Land Cruiser* is enough to construct a fully-stocked school or hospital in remote villages. Some become womanizers and hook up one woman after another, which is their norm and a political fashion in the city. Youths must be different if they are prepared to shape the country into a South Sudan that we all dream of achieving through peace and harmony. We should distance ourselves from our current politicians whom I have nicknamed *the most dangerous weapons of mass destruction*, and from the *grocers* who flaunt their *belly fashion* to appear more responsible and politicized.

Politicians in South Sudan have one common belief - being in positions of authority not to serve the common person, but to enrich their already massive tummies. The same belief applies nationwide, from states, counties, payams to bomas. Please note it is not my intention to criticize the civil servants who work tirelessly to serve the government on a monthly minimum wage and other few politicians who work tirelessly for a better South Sudan. There are a few of whom we hope to multiply and triple. There is a need for being politically informed to comprehend that the lack of good governance is causing us all to suffer, both in the public and private sectors. The dilemma in South Sudan's political philosophy is the creation of a government department or office staffed by people from only one tribe which alone diminishes the spirit of national cohesion among the country's 64 ethnic groups. For example, in some national ministries and state departments, senior positions have been assigned to tribesmen from a single ethnic group which is unfair as it suggests that there is no one qualified among other tribes to hold these positions. The conundrum is that such appointments often lead to the formation of tribal cliques in which all staff use the same mother tongue, rather than the official language which is English.

In late 2019, I worked at both the Ministry of Petroleum and the Ministry of Finance where every official talked to me in *Dinka*! Is this the description of South Sudan we dreamt of? Of course not. The trend is the same in ministries headed by someone from *Nuer* and *Cholok* tribes and it still goes on within the current *RTGoNU*, where tribalist officials are fighting to retain their ministries. The new 35 Ministers of the *R-TGoNU* are supposed to provide their *First 100 Days* working plans, but one thing I am certain of is that politics is a *rat race*, you chase a position until you get it despite the incompetency and inability to get anything done. Political alignment, allegiance, and loyalty are the core values in securing for yourself a senior government position like a Minister or a Permanent secretary. Hence, it all depends on how hard you campaign for it using all the lobbying skills at your disposal. That's all right, congratulations to those who make it to the throne of the protective political executive!

However, there is still a chance for *President Salva Kiir, First Vice President Dr. Riek Machar,* and *Vice Presidents Gen. Taban Deng, Dr. Wani Igga, Mama Rebecca Nyandeng Garang,* and *Hussein Abdelbagi* to propose the *First 100 Days* working plan approach to all the Ministers to produce concrete strategies for running their assigned offices and presenting their contributions or achievements in the implementation of the peace agreement. The appointed Ministers are obliged to publicly present the plans to the revitalized transitional parliament with a live stream to the people of South Sudan through the national television. This step can help to win people's faith and trust in the transitional government in its resolve to implement peace resolutions or steering a new approach to sustainable development in South Sudan. Ultimately, the presidency can evaluate the performance of the 35 Cabinet Ministers in implementing their *First 100 Days* working plans to weigh their competency and vision for national development. We need hardworking Ministers to propel South Sudan to prosperity and sustainable development rather than the useless politicians who roam around their offices aimlessly in fancy suits and red ties. I hope that every *(young)* aspiring leader gets a strong head start on what he or she needs to do to transform the country into a developed nation that values education and competence.

In particular, due to the *Oyee* Party's policy of governing the country with weapons and the military, academic degrees were not considered because the SPLM regarded those who studied in Sudan as traitors who chose to study from the adversary's territory. For this reason, it is more appropriate and acceptable for you to enter into any public office, present yourself with a gun, and ask for any bureaucratic position of your liking without academic credentials or professional experience. The usual slogan was *Belaid Da Ma Be Shahaadad,* literally translated *This country will not be liberated by certificates,* forgetting that *Dr. John Garang De Mabior,* a P.h.D. holder championed for the new vision of *Sudan Jadeid* - the *New Sudan* until his sudden death in 2005 after the signing of the *CPA.* I admire his call for taking the city into the village because it was a call from a well-educated leader who had a strong vision of transforming the largely archaic country into a modern one. Such a patriotic spirit is still lacking in the current *SPLM/A* - the fragmented *Oyee* Party. Many other *SPLM/A* members in the military and high command are also well-educated, and it is difficult to say where the idea and slogan of managing the country with weapons and militia-mindsets came from. We have been conditioned to believe that it is only politicians and military men who can solve our problems, but at some point, we must stay alert to bear in mind that our politicians are the ones who created our problem and remain our biggest problem to date.

Lethal Propaganda Tools

Divisive, destructive, and disparaging!

Media perception in South Sudan has taken a wrong course as it is mainly considered a tool that produces fake news, promotes tribalism, and social evils among the youth. This was particularly witnessed in the violence that followed the *SPLM/A House Downfall (the 2013 – 2020 Civil War)* because of the irresponsible reporting by various media houses who rallied tribalistic sentiments among the populace. Then, based on their agenda-setting theorem, the media outlets spewed hatred and warfare among the South Sudanese, pitting one tribe against another *(i.e. Nuer vs. Dinka)*. This manipulation and exploitation of the already fragile ethnic divisions fostered support for a violent conflict that served only the interests of the leaders of kleptocratic networks known as *"political parties"* run by our pot-bellied *Uncles* as the self-declared few elites and heroes of liberation.

The war in South Sudan and its coverage by local media has once again highlighted its role in drumming up both support and attention to modern warfare, given its ability to fuel conflict through manipulation. Such intensity of media coverage was never witnessed in the half-century war with Sudan. Not only mainstream media, but even social media is an active public rallying tool that fuels hostilities between families, communities, tribes, and the nation by exaggerating local conflicts. Using mass media as an additional weapon of war became rampant during the *SPLM/A* War with Sudan *(1983–2005)* and it reached a level of complexity in the *SPLM/A* House's Downfall *(2013–2020)*. In particular, using social media *(Facebook, Twitter, blogs, Instagram, and websites)* and news agencies to transmit and manage information and disinformation has become so alarming in recent years, exposing the internal strife within the *SPLM/A* party that expanded into widespread hostilities across the country. War by the media is classified as low-intensity conflict, alongside subversion, rebellion, insurrection, and psychological sabotage.

Propaganda theorists say that in a political war against the media, a man should be considered a primary target, and just as in military warfare, the human mind remains the focal point. Without bullets, a human mind becomes easily putrefied once it is programmed with nepotism and tribalism without necessarily receiving bullets, and the first causality, here, is always the *truth*. The use of propaganda and disinformation during the 2013 war was widespread and effective in achieving its intended political and tribal purposes. The warring parties and their protagonists succeeded in sustaining the impression that it was a planned war, coup d'etat, political exclusion, dictatorship, or civil war - a claim disputed by all but resulted in negligible human fatalities throughout the country.

To this end, the widespread use of the media in press briefings was framed by video footage of war scenes proving each party's defensive advantages, while military spokespeople blatantly discussed the human cost of the war in terms of the number of enemy troops captured and villages burned down - a tragedy widely praised by loyal social media followers. Not an hour goes by without someone posting or commenting on social media about the military, militias, violence, or weapons. The same trend is prevalent on the mainstream media as hate is wantonly spewed. One example is a daily program *SPLM/A's SSTV* hosted by the Military Director for Information and Public Relations *Brig. Gen. Malak Ayuen Ajok* on SSBC to discuss and boast the SSPDF's military supremacy, especially the possession of advanced weapons of warfare. Such biased shows are detrimental to national development and growth and hence should be replaced by programs that promote nationalism rather than nepotism, tribalism, conflict, and corruption.

For the young people who want to join the media industry in South Sudan, I believe that the information technology revolution has enabled the media to have a much greater impact on people's perceptions, which is why some use it as a platform for seeking change and reforms. Scholars call it the fourth branch of government which is true especially if it is run responsibly and professionally. In that case, it can serve as a tool that can save the nation from destructive misinformation and bring to the public the incumbent politicians on their knees foraging for appropriate explanations. There are many instances in which even high-ranking figures, including the president, have appeared in the state media before the people of South Sudan to refute viral news about political issues or the country's unknown challenges. The media, if used to advance a worthy common agenda, can be a vital force in bringing together the leaders and those being led to a common ground for advancing national interests. It is therefore imperative to look more closely at the complicated relationship between the government and the media and to understand the former's role during conflicts.

More recently South Sudan's use — or rather abuse of the media to outwit its people during the 2013 SPLM House's Downfall is a case in point in which the state misused the media as a propaganda tool to divide the country along political and tribal lines. The question here is: *who needs whom most? Do the media need the government or does the government need the media?* But the answer is not so simple because, throughout history, the two institutions have always been at loggerheads. The government is always popular, but it is at its best in political organizations and functions that have an enormous amount of incompetence, and if the government makes mistakes and loses direction, it even becomes hard to notice.

The government operates in a homogeneous environment - a closed culture that can be hostile to outsiders. At times, the news media are often unpopular with the brass as they are bound to function independently, without rules, regulations, or even a Code of Conduct except for some that are self-imposed. The media has its share of bad apples, scoundrels, incompetents, and greedy vultures tarnishing the industry's name, especially through yellow journalism. But at its best, the media offers a vital service to the nation that we cannot get anywhere else, which is one of the pillars of the state to which the people of South Sudan are subscribed. For those with privileges of internet access, social media has proved vital in obtaining real-time information to keep abreast of what is happening in all corners of the country.

In general, however, the media has been abused by both the state, opportunists, and troublemakers. Regardless, the media yearns for the freedom to freely operate without restrictions, in addition to the unrestrained access to state information to enable it to execute its work as the fourth estate of the nation by bringing their stories quickly to the citizens of the nation. The government, however, wants to tighten its grip on the media through regulation and control, but the media fears that the government might suppress balanced news coverage in favor of fine-tuning the regime's reputation or covering up its blunders, but these are fundamental differences that will never change.

Sometimes the government and the patriotic media have cooperated harmoniously, but usually, hostility clouds their relationship as the media yearns for balanced news, while the government has its polished side that it wants the media to portray, and, above all, both need public support. The media can tell their story and if there are rapports and an understanding, they can tell it well and effectively. During the war, when there is a life-or-death struggle for the military, patriotism comes to their aid, both personally and institutionally, instinctively, and through their extensive training. The civilian media lacks such training, and nothing personal is at stake. Self-aggrandizement seems the raison d'être of most people, but war times are good and profitable for the media business.

Probably every conflict is fought on at least two war fronts - on the battlefield and in people's minds through propaganda. In a tug of war for public support, both the good and the bad sides can often be guilty of misleading their people through distortions, exaggerations, subjectivity, inaccuracy, and even invention to gain approval and a sense of legitimacy. In times of war or during war preparation, messages of extremities and hatred, combined with emotions of honor and righteousness play together to deliver powerful propaganda for a cause where the first casualty when war breaks out is the absence of a true story.

During the SPLM House's Downfall (2013 – 2020), the media reported thousands of killings, possible attacks, and the recapture of megacities or relaying of strongly held areas – all for the sole purpose of propagandizing the warmongers to promote violence and weaponry. I strongly advise all young journalists and the budding media professionals to champion truthfulness, objectivity, and accountability - the media should be a platform for promoting unity, diversity, and investment opportunities in South Sudan, not a vehicle for the heat-sapping rhetoric, nepotism, and tribalism that has driven the country into the abyss. Unfortunately to heed this advice is a huge risk in South Sudan for many journalists and media owners because the few who have boldly spoken out the truth over the years have been subjected to state harassment, imprisonment, and death.

Democracy thrives best when the government takes legitimate steps to preserve its secrets, while the press knows and fulfills what is in the best interest of the public and the nation. In propaganda posters, illustrations and headlines, malicious stereotypes are contested; the population would be amazed to ascertain how they and their leaders are portrayed from the other side. But the myth has stirred public opinion at a critical moment about the need for war, yet the media should be a partner in eradicating war out of South Sudan. The sad truth is that government propaganda is packaged so skillfully to prepare the citizens for war, and it is probable that the regime and its warmongers do not want a truthful, objective, and balanced reporting about the state of the nation's affairs.

In such situations, the media is supposed to provide the public with precise information that also leaves room for a second thought before absorbing or rejecting propaganda that is not only about war but also about other aspects of life, including the political, economic, and social aspects. An *Institute for Propaganda Analysis* needs to be set up urgently to educate South Sudanese citizens about the widespread type of political and military propaganda that has stalled the country's development and growth. The connotation is that those in the authority must be held accountable for the good of the nation, and that is where the mainstream media comes in as the mainstay of functioning democracy and transparency through their role as a watchdog for the public's interest.

Through the skillful and steadfast use of propaganda, people can be misled to consider paradise as hell, tribalism as nationalism and the most miserable kind of life portrayed as paradise. The primitive simplicity of their minds impels them to easily prey on a big lie than a small one. With propaganda, you don't need facts per se, you just need the most appealing facts to be presented. If these facts make sense to the audience, they don't need the kind of evidence that is usually presented in a courtroom. The smart way to keep people passive and obedient is to strictly limit the spectrum of acceptable opinions, but allow a vigorous debate within that spectrum while encouraging even the more critical and dissident views. This gives people the feeling that free-thinking abounds, while the assumptions of the system are constantly reinforced by the limits of the range of debate which works well among the educated people. Studies show that among the more educated sections of the population, government propaganda about the war is now accepted wholeheartedly and unchallenged. One convincing reason why propaganda often works better on the educated than on the uneducated is that educated people read more, and so they receive more propaganda to keep feeding on the brainwashing diet. We need to tell the facts, good or bad before others litter the media with disinformation and distortions, which they will certainly continue to do. We must challenge the accepted rule of thumb in wars of showing only pictures of dead enemies. At times, casualty figures were manipulated and reported with low numbers to avoid embarrassment, while those of the enemy were often exaggerated to strike a winning tone in the hearts of their loyalists. Defeats were simply omitted or delayed in the coverage, sometimes declared a tactical retreat or strategic evacuation.

Gender Mainstreaming

In nation-building, no gender is left behind

Gender mainstreaming was first proposed in 1985 at the *Third World Conference on Women* in Kenya. Since then, the idea was integrated for implementation within the *United Nations* development community. Gender mainstreaming was formally featured in 1995 at the *Fourth World Conference on Women* in Beijing, China, and was cited in the resulting document the *Beijing Platform for Action*. The *United Nations Economic and Social Council* formally defined this concept as a process for assessing the impact of any planned action, including laws, policies, or programs on women and men in all areas and at all levels. It is a strategy to highlight the concerns and experiences of women and men as an integral dimension of the design, implementation, monitoring, and evaluation of policies and programs in all political, economic, and social areas so that women and men benefit equally and inequality does not persist. The ultimate objective is to achieve gender equality and balance in all spheres of life.

The legacy of the conflict in South Sudan is marred by gender exploitation *(especially women as the most affected victims)*, widespread poverty, destruction of physical capital and infrastructure, disenfranchised state institutions, and millions of lost and displaced people. Despite the apparent improvement in the state of the nation since the signing of the CPA in 2005 until the formation of RTGoNU in 2020, South Sudan's socio-economic indicators are still weak and gender disparities are extreme. Although education and health indicators are improving, they remain among the worst in the region, especially for the nation's girls and women. Despite the legal provisions that protect against discrimination based on one's gender, respect for human rights is still lacking considering the prevalent policies that predominantly favor men over women, and the persistent cultural norms like bridal traditions and early marriage. Economic barriers to young men and women are enormous, and without targeted attention, they threaten to undermine efforts to promote inclusive growth and broader internal stability. *Gender-based violence (GBV)* is rife in South Sudan as it renders almost all our homes unsafe.

Affirmative action quotas which stipulate that *thirty-five percent* of government posts be occupied by women are positive steps towards moderate political participation, but these quotas are yet to be achieved as there is still a significant gap between the presence in government and active effective participation in government. In the context of this chapter, gender refers to the socially constructed roles and relationships between women and men. Variables influence these roles, including age, race, class, and ethnicity, and change over time depending on learning levels and evolving contexts. Diagnosing and analyzing gender inequalities has important implications for poverty reduction and sustainable development, especially in the context of persistent instability. Identifying and understanding the unique barriers and opportunities faced by men, women, boys, and girls helps to ensure that interventions, project activities, and analytical work promote the equitable realization of economic, political, and social achievements. Women and girls in South Sudan are exposed to many social injustices that violate their natural rights and freedom. Some of these infringements are broadly explained below:

Gender and Sexual-Based Violence (GSBV)

Women and girls in South Sudan are highly vulnerable to widespread gender and sexual-based violence. Countless among a South Sudanese wife's domestic duties include caring for the family, performing mundane tasks such as collecting firewood, cultivating the garden, and caring for her husbands, relatives, and children. Besides, physical assault and rape by armed men are commonplace. Their haunting encounter with deluded gunmen makes our women too scared to venture outside of the safety of their homesteads on their own - whether day or night, and this is increasingly causing frictions within families and local communities. We can never be an inclusive nation if one gender feels too scared to move on their own for fear of being sexually abused or physically exploited. We can put an end to this by applying strict laws to punish the perpetrators for the crimes committed against vulnerable women and young girls.

Bride price business and forced marriages

In the South Sudanese context, for one to have a companion, there must be something culturally paid by the groom's family to the bride's family. This payment is in exchange for the bride and is called the bride price. Bride price *(dowry)* or bridewealth can be in the form of property, livestock, goods, money, or any form of wealth among others. As insane as it sounds, it is not the kind of marriage arrangement that God intended for his children on earth but to some cultures, this is a profitable venture that diminishes the social self-esteem of our young girls and women.

It is taboo for a man in his forties to have no companion simply because he cannot afford a dowry for paying as a bride price, at least his family or community must organize for him. Nowadays, marriage is no longer determined by love, but by how rich a person is, and in many South Sudanese communities, the price of the bride can be revealed in the value of goods the groom's family hands over to the bride's family. This involves the delivery of livestock, such as cattle or goats, to the father of the future wife, and when the dowry is paid or settled, the bride must leave her parents' home and live in unison with her husband in a manner reminiscent of the biblical teachings on marriage. But if God was to ask for a dowry, Adam would have been the first to command Eve in the Garden of Eden.

Bride price is widely practiced all over the nation as it is a key part of all South Sudanese marriages without which a man and woman's union can never be officially and legally recognized. It is difficult to break such a practice because it is a crucial part of the cultural identity that is widely praised and recognized. Since it is a lucrative business for the impoverished families of potential brides, today's bride price is higher than what South Sudan's poorest men can afford. That is why these unfortunate men resort to kidnapping women and girls for wives, raping and impregnating their suitors, and sometimes later abandoning them. The exorbitant bride price and forced wedlocks render the marriage institution to lose its original meaning of being a pure union of true love between two consenting adult partners. Today, it is one of the most lucrative businesses to obtain quick money at the expense of our sisters or daughters, who are denied their right to choose their partners.

Today's dowry has more than tripled what it used to be and given its lucrativeness, in the developed countries it would be termed as untaxed transactions. The bride's family demands whatever they want to be paid by the bridegroom's family. Some have gone to the extent of demanding an airplane which sounds preposterous, but it shows how South Sudanese families often go off track in their ridiculous demands for riches in exchange for a soul. Such demands often provoke anger and discontent among South Sudanese communities, especially the young men hence deciding to marry from other tribes from where a more affordable bride price will be asked. These young men are not doing this out of love but they are just looking for a cheaper bride price deal. A high dowry can lead to dowry violence, *leftover* female ideologies, abortion, deliberate euthanasia, marital passivity of young men, and the disintegration of the social fabric that holds South Sudan together.

There are also many cases of exorbitant dowry, but because there is no love, the marriage breaks up after which the bride's parents must pay back the groom's dowry. Why are we humiliating our girls in this way, treating them like a transactable commodity? This is pure cultural madness! The question that needs to be answered is: Why are local leaders indifferent instead of addressing this problem? Fast-forward, the high bride price tag frames our daughters into marketable merchandise. Not only that, but they are also treated as property, objects of masculine pleasure, and more tragically, as a child-producing machine. The exorbitant bride price often leads to communal conflicts in case one community or family cannot afford the extravagant bride price asked by the other community or family. This ultimately leads to unnecessary loss of innocent lives and conflicts between communities because a particular family must raid the surrounding villages for livestock to be paid as bride price for their young man to marry the girl of his dreams.

The groom will mistreat and physically abuse the bride, seeing her as his property, which he bought at a heavy cost. Where the husband does not pay the bride price, he will have no respect from the in-laws. Sometimes, when the girl is highly educated, her bride price will be inflated, because the amount her parents spent on her education will have to be reimbursed. For this reason, educated youths do not like highly educated girls, because they assume that they will compete with them for household and family supremacy. Most male graduates prefer girls who are brought in from the villages as wives. Please, young boys, let us stop enslaving our girls as pets for us to subdue in control, but let them go to school and contribute to the development of the country. An educated woman can assist you in managing the house affairs, including meeting the home operational expenses, maintaining good health for your children, in addition to offering upbuilding advice, guidance, and consultation in everyday matters.

Don't get it twisted, the uneducated are also mothers and leaders at their own pace and their contribution is unwavering both at the home, community, and national levels. In my opinion, adequate education for girls should be promoted without these general social barriers. Women in politics seem to be more recycled and overused by the men, and this should not be the trend for our dear young people. We need to get the country moving forward and ahead with a gender balance system in a way that empowers women to become bold and competent decision-makers. Most young South Sudanese girls simply focus on creating fashionable characters on Facebook and Instagram by feigning happiness, trendy styles, and enjoyment without focusing on what matters most. Even if *thirty-five percent* of public service slots are given to women according to the Affirmative Action and no one is claiming and advocating for it, then I am sure men will one day wear skirts to occupy those slots.

Back to marriage, in an attempt to get hold of the bride's wealth, the young people have struggled to attain it even to the extent of engaging in delinquent practices including robbery and selling their parents' properties or communal land. In rare cases, the girl elopes with the boy to be impregnated by him, to make the dowry easier and cheaper. Due to the exorbitant bride price, sometimes our beautiful sisters are coerced into marrying men they do not like, thus leading to forced and abusive marriages, and for this reason, husbands do not value the dignity of their wives. In most cases, couples who cannot afford to pay the bride price resort to cohabitation, others go for illegal marriages, while some naughty girls end into prostitution. The bride price culture lowers our young girls' human dignity, intrudes in their academic careers, and renders a deeply sexist attitude that objectifies women, which altogether compromises their future. A woman who supports her husband during the marriage is culturally unacceptable, but few girls do so in secret. Bingo, these girls will one day champion for the rights of South Sudanese women, but we must encourage marriages based on love and not material wealth and lust. Do well to remember that marriages founded on true love have the perfect environment for raising upright children.

Representation by women

During the formation of the *R-TGoNU*, representation by women was and is still an issue in the governance and civil structures of South Sudan. According to a report published by some media in 2020, the *SPLM* women's caucus called on *President Salva Kiir* to appoint at least three women to governorship positions. The revitalized agreement indicated that a *thirty-five percent* quota would represent women in all the newly formed structures. But *President Kiir* violated the agreement and brushed off the *SPLM* women's caucus demands. Their recommendation that *thirty-five percent* of all appointments be made to women was blatantly disregarded. This was not the first time women in politics have complained about misrepresentation as previous requests by women in *SPLM-IO*, *SSOA*, *OPP*, and other political entities were ignored. Women have immensely contributed to the attainment of sustainable peace, right since the outbreak of the 2013 civil war. However, they have paid the heaviest price, and they are still fighting for legitimate representation in all the three arms of the government - the executive, legislature, and judiciary.

Promises are good to make and their public proclamation is quite demanding in a way that sometimes requires leaders to sacrifice their efforts as well as all the resources at their disposal. Nonetheless, the zeal to deliver on the promises is becoming a rock to be turned around. Why is it difficult for our leaders to fulfill what has already been said in the ears of all those who have heard it? As we speak, women are left to complain about what the parties promised them in the *R-ARCSS* document. Women now believe that they were duped into believing the politicians' fake promises following the recent male-dominated appointment of Governors by the President on *29th June 2020*. In *February 2019*, *President Kiir* approved the *thirty-five percent* Affirmative Action for women representation, arguing that there would be no reason to reduce the gesture but if need be, instead it should be added onto. However, since governors were appointed, none of these decisions were followed upon, according to several civil society activists. The *SPLM-in-charge* was supposed to appoint two female governors while the *SPLM/A- in-opposition* had to appoint one female governor which the latter observed. Nevertheless, I am in favor of greater participation and representation of women in a prosperous and peaceful South Sudan.

Women involvement in war and peace

The idea of integrating women's views and voices in the peace process is slowly gaining momentum. Nowadays, women are perceived in one way or another as a force for peace and harmony, as educators, and carers, but in some primitive sections of our society this is intolerable, and such a repudiation is a cultural construct rooted in sexist values. However, if these cultural stereotypes can be used to promote peace, then they can bring benefits to women and men alike. Women have suffered terribly in all previous wars, and they still suffer from poverty, inequality, discrimination, and sexual abuse even in relatively calm times.

During conflicts, all these elements become aggravated. Women carry the most agricultural burden in this country unassisted and are the ones involved in feeding our nation, but all we repay them is inflicting more physical and emotional pain on them. War usually means even more workloads and responsibilities for women, whether they are at home and their husbands have left, abandoned them, been drafted, died, or driven out of their homes - women always carry the extra burden as they must look after their children. Women in female-led households must assume the exclusive responsibility for caring for the remaining family members, perhaps supplemented by orphaned members of the extended family. They could find themselves solely responsible for growing food and earning an income,especially through petty trade. They may have to venture into new trades which are risky as they must travel far away to obtain merchandise.

While liberating women from the constraints of domestic work and agriculture may be a relief-providing experience for some, it is simply an additional burden and risk for many. Older daughters may be forced out of school to look after the younger siblings and hence their future becomes sacrificed for the immediate family. Women who are poor and in dire need of food or money for themselves and their children are exposed to exploitation and sexual abuse. They can be exploited economically by traders who buy their merchandise at below-average prices, or by farmers who employ women labor force at below-average work rates, and sometimes refuse to pay them. Young women are left with no choice but to become commercial sex workers or to bind themselves to many male partners to survive, which are most dominant in urban contexts.

Women are prone to sexual abuse, particularly when they are beyond the safe confines of their families, villages, clans, or communities as they become extremely vulnerable to rape. This carries with it the risk of HIV infections, and soldiers are among those at the greatest risk of HIV transmission and other sexually transmitted diseases. Women exposed to these vices are also prone to unwanted pregnancies, which leads to abortion, stigma, and lifetime trauma. For wartime poor women, life consists of trying to manage multiple risks as nothing is certain since there is no reliable guide for how to act in such situations. Many women face unacceptable choices every day: whether to plant or cook maize seeds to feed their children; whether to take a long journey or risk landmines on a shorter one; whether to risk HIV infection by accepting or renouncing sexual favors in exchange for a job; and whether to risk it and work in male-dominated jobs or become beggars on the streets.

Of course, men also suffer from war, especially poor men and young people, because in most wars it is men who suffer most death or disability during combat. Widows and orphans may be suffering, but they are still alive. But in many wars, civilian casualties outnumber military ones, and women may suffer disproportionately from the combined effects of social vulnerability, sexual abuse, displacement, and hardship. Usually, men also suffer most from food crises. For every famine and refugee crisis for which statistical information is available, death rates were higher for men than for women. This applies, with a few exceptions, to all age groups from young male children to the elderly.

Women under customary law

Another major obstacle to gender equality in South Sudan is the primacy of customary law, which in many cases has a more significant impact on women's legal status than the legal framework outlined in the constitution. Legal pluralism is a defining feature of the legal framework in South Sudan, as customary law coexists with legal systems. Many articles in the Transitional Constitution enshrine the legitimacy of the

Gender Mainstreaming

customary courts in the South Sudanese society and customary courts are largely responsible for the administration of justice in the ten states and administrative regions. Customary laws vary by region, community, and ethnic group, and are not codified to adapt to changing situations over time. Legal issues affecting women in South Sudan, including marriage, land inheritance, property rights, and domestic disputes which are all often referred to ordinary courts for judgment and determination. However, the customary laws common in South Sudan often contradict international human rights principles and the rights of women, girls, and children.

Traditional courts are dominated by male tribal chiefs who hold conservative views on women's rights and roles in South Sudanese society. As a result, court rulings often reflect and uphold the deeply entrenched patriarchal norms that fundamentally disadvantage women. For example, the 2008 *Penal Code* contains several provisions that criminalize the various forms of gender-based violence including assault, incest, rape, female genital mutilation, abduction, adultery, and acts of gross indecency. Among the provisions, sexual intercourse with persons under the age of 18 is prohibited and considered child defilement. The 2008 *Child Act* similarly prohibits marriage with anyone under the age of *eighteen* and articulates the need for mutual consent. Early, often forced marriages, however, remain widely practiced and hence unlikely to be punished under the customary laws. Although physical assault is illegal under the *Penal Code*, traditional practices often regard domestic violence against women as permissible as a husband has the right to *discipline* or teach his wife a lesson. Such is the level of absurdity in our customary laws.

Women in human development

South Sudan's socio-economic indicators continue to be among the lowest in the world. Estimates of maternal mortality in 2006 were *2,054 per 100,000 inhabitants*, which is among the highest in the world and indicates poor health care for women with high fertility rates[8]. In 2006, young women between the ages of *fifteen* and *nineteen* were more likely to die during childbirth than finish primary school. Female-led households, which account for almost *twenty-nine percent* of the

---
[8]South Sudan Household Survey (2006).

population, are among the poorest, with *fifty-six percent* falling below the poverty line as compared with *forty-eight percent* of male-led households. Consequently, high illiteracy and the lack of education continue to be a major obstacle to improvements in human capital development in South Sudan as they limit access to opportunities across a variety of the political, social, and economic spectrum. To meet this challenge, development partners repeatedly recommended the inclusion of adult/functional literacy components in all projects under preparation. Investment in strategies to improve access to higher education levels should as well be prioritized.

Women in livelihood development

Women in South Sudan are greatly constrained by the scarcity of income-generating activities partly caused by years of overdependence on humanitarian aid. Persistent insecurity, problematic resource management, particularly the unfair land distribution system, have limited women's ability to participate fully in livelihood development through the predominant agriculture - a sector that is still practiced at the subsistence level. Consequently, South Sudan remains heavily dependent on humanitarian food and relief aid, as well as food imports from neighboring countries including Uganda, Sudan, and Kenya. One of the development priorities for South Sudan should, therefore, be the diversification of the non-oil economy sector, with a particular focus on the rapid expansion of agricultural production.

Such diversification must be achieved in part by improving infrastructure networks *(roads, storage facilities, markets)*, technology transfer and acquisition, integrated communication networks in rural areas, and improved access to agricultural land. Increasing access to financial services and improving the policy and regulatory climate for businesses must as well be prioritized. Obstacles to greater participation of women in income-generating activities must be uprooted. These include insufficient childcare and support opportunities, illiteracy and the lack of access to formal education, insufficient opportunities for technical training *(hands-on skills)*, and the lack of entrepreneurial skills, lack of access to financial services, and the lack of access to production factors including land, markets, and inputs like seeds and farm implements. The primary statutory texts that explicitly address gender disparities in South Sudan include the *Transitional Constitution of South Sudan* and its attendant *Bill* of Rights, the 2008 Penal Code, and the 2008 Child Act (UNHCR 2011). The Bill of Rights of South Sudan's Transitional Constitution, as well as the previous Comprehensive Peace Agreement of 2005 and the Interim Constitution of South Sudan, all contain provisions that prohibit any forms of discrimination on the grounds of sex or gender.

More specifically, Article 16 (Rights of Women) in the Transitional Constitution states the following;

★ Women shall be accorded full and equal dignity of the person with men;
★ Women shall have the right to equal pay for equal work and other related benefits with men;
★ Women shall have the right to participate equally with men in public life; and

All levels of government shall:

★ Promote women's participation in public life and their representation in the legislative and executive organs by at least *thirty-five percent* as an affirmative action to redress the imbalances created by history, customs, and traditions;
★ Enact laws to combat harmful customs and traditions which undermine the dignity and status of women; and
★ Provide maternity and child care, and medical care for pregnant and lactating women
★ Women shall have the right to own property and share in the estates of their deceased husbands together with any surviving legal heir of the deceased.

Accordingly, South Sudan's constitution provides several important safeguards against gender discrimination, including quotas for political representation at all levels of government, access to land and the right to inherit property, provisions on maternity and child care, and economic equity. A selection of articles within the *Bill of Rights* that provide for equality and the preservation of human, economic, social, and cultural rights include the right to life, the right to found a family *(Article 15)*, and the right to personal liberty *(Article 12)*. Others include gender equality *(Article 14)*, rights of the child *(Article 17)*, rights to education *(Article 29)*, rights to public health care *(Article 31)*, rights to ethnic and cultural communities *(Article 33)*, and rights to own property *(Article28)*. However, the implementation and enforcement of these rights remain a huge challenge. While the *thirty-five percent* quota of women in national and legislative assemblies signals an important step towards gender equality in decision-making, the presence of women in the political system does not necessarily imply active participation and legislation.

Despite the significant gains particularly at the highest ministerial levels which meet the minimum *thirty-five percent* threshold for political participation, all other sectors of the new government have not yet achieved the women's quota, particularly at the state and lower administrative levels. Few women have the financial means to pay the electoral fees for running as candidates and to campaign locally or nationally during elections. Women who manage to compete for political seats are confronted by the deep-seated patriarchal norms that do not support women's assumption of leadership positions in public life, but it is extremely difficult to win and maintain the confidence of the electorate. Most women who succeed in being elected to political positions may still not have the formal education or technical experience to effectively carry out their mandate and duties. Even if they have the necessary experience, elected women still face prejudice and intimidation from their male colleagues who try to discourage/belittle their contributions to public service. Nevertheless, the demand for meaningful participation of women through gender mainstreaming must be made loud and clear.

Boosting Youth Productivity

Elect leaders who can keep jobs in the country

C hoose the right leaders to sustain jobs in South Sudan through the creation of opportunities for locals to attain self-developed capitals and revenues. Such leaders should empower innovators and SME owners who can supply the market with their goods and services. It is painful that the country's institutions of higher learning keep churning out hundreds of thousands of graduates, but these are automatically rendered jobless due to bad governance and the absence of employment opportunities from both the private and public sectors. One of the reasons for the excessive unemployment is that far too many young people across the country graduate without relevant skills that are employable, which means that investing in education is currently not working. In general, at least *sixty percent* of Africa's unemployed are youth, according to the World Bank, and many are resorting to crime, conflicts, or the often-perilous migration journey across the Mediterranian Sea to Europe in search of greener pastures.

A similar scenario unfolds in South Sudan, where the hopeless youth are either wandering on the streets of cities, joining criminal gangs to rob people, or being recruited into militias to wage wars. A Chinese man once said, *"Whoever asks is a fool for five minutes, but whoever does not ask remains a fool forever."* We all know that South Sudan's economy is experiencing negative per capita income growth, and many sectors are suffering from harsh economic conditions. We know that employment should be a top priority for the current transitional government of national unity and progressive governance if it leads to the development and meaningful participation of youth in nation-building. I intend to propose an approach that takes into account the government's objective and strategy to create job opportunities for young people to try and increase the available employment opportunities. This is impossible without first finding a solution to challenges that have brought our nation a bad reputation. South Sudan's economy is one of Africa's weakest and is among the world's least developed countries, with poor infrastructure, and having the highest maternal mortality and illiteracy rates in the world. Most of the country's villages have no electricity, roads, and clean running water, and the country's infrastructure is poor, with only twenty-five percent of its total road network currently paved.

All hope is not lost as the government has embarked on repairing some broken infrastructure, including roads, hospitals, markets, and schools despite attempts to derail them by corrupt officials. The ongoing electricity and water extension would have been a positive step towards diversifying the country's economy, however, the bureaucratic system connives with foreign companies to exaggerate the costs with a mission of taking a lion's share through dubious contracts. Expensive diesel generators produce electricity which is accessible by only two percent of the nation's population which leaves the remainder in darkness. I think the current electricity distribution covers only the metropolitan region of Juba and the surrounding area, although its costs are high in comparison to the individual income per month, and worse still, the utility company does not employ locals who are robbed of the opportunity to enjoy working for the betterment of their country.

There has been a significant investment by Chinese companies in the country, particularly in infrastructure and energy, but very few local young people are recruited because most of our youths lack the requisite technical know-how, which is why Chinese engineers, surveyors, surveyors, and managers are brought in big numbers. I dispute this as a *'big Chinese-made lie'* because we have a substantial number of young talented South Sudanese engineering graduates from prominent universities both here and abroad who are now sitting idly at home. The few South Sudanese youths working on these projects either bribed their way into being recruited or were connected via strong recommendations from the pot-bellied *Uncles* within the government and are affiliated to these companies.

The government needs to do something about the recruitment policies of oil companies. The question is, when will our able-bodied and highly-skilled young engineers be employed in the various oil companies that operate here? For how long shall we remain dependent on foreign engineers to extract our oil while sidelining our competent graduates? The answer to these questions can be found in Henry

Kissinger's famous quote: *"Whoever controls your oil as food controls your national policy and your people."* And that explains why foreigners are in charge of our country because they control oil exploration, oil drilling, production, and export.

As young people who care deeply about the future of this nation, we should work with the government to develop a workable youth empowerment strategy through the provision of employment opportunities in various public projects and government departments. This can empower us to competently manage our national resources, including the oil which should be extracted by our competent engineers, rather than favoring foreigners who do not care about developing this nation. Meanwhile, around *ninety percent* of consumer goods are imported from neighboring countries, mainly Uganda, Kenya, and Sudan thus stifling the local market with cheap imports. We need to strengthen our resolve to achieve a self-sustaining nation that is developed by the South Sudanese themselves so that we do not suffer the fate that Kissinger's quotation above heralds. We should not always rely on foreign aid which is an insult to our social being as a country with rich resources that can be used for the common good of its people as it will further derail our expectations of a country that we want.

I hope that with such enthusiasm, including the completion of the ongoing road infrastructure development, electricity, and water pipeline, more employment opportunities for young people can be made available. In addition to the state contributions to support young entrepreneurs, the setting up of attractive incentives for bringing in foreign direct investments can also increase the employment rate for our young people. This is the only way to divert their minds from idleness, abstaining from bloody politics, and communal violence. There is little guilt, however, as landlocked South Sudan's industry and infrastructure development are severely underdeveloped, given that the government made excuses in the 2013 struggle in which poverty was widespread among all communities after several decades of civil war in search of an independent state. Ongoing conflicts within the new nation are disrupting our economic growth as many investors have left the country, leading to a sharp rise in unemployment among young people, especially the youthful women. The vast majority of the population is dependent on humanitarian aid, with only a few communities reliant on subsistence farming, especially in the relatively peaceful areas.

Nevertheless, South Sudan has an abundance of natural resources, with some of the richest agricultural environments in the region, owing to its fertile soils and abundant water supply. At present, the agricultural sector can support between 10 and 20 million cattle, but because of the almost daily intercommunal violence mostly by the youths, this is impossible. The outbreak of conflicts in December 2013, combined with dwindling crude oil production and prices, significantly reduced our GDP. The COVID-19 outbreak exacerbated the problem by crippling all economic activities in the country. The nation's youths have every fundamental right to participate in the country's decision and policy-making as enshrined by the law provided under the agreement on the Resolution of the Conflicts in the Republic of South Sudan. I call upon our country's politicians to understand that politics should not be turned into a means for self-aggrandizing attainment of wealth and prosperity, but through noble politics, they should serve the public interest by ensuring inclusive access to health, education, markets, electricity, water, and security to everyone regardless of their tribal, religious, or political affiliations.

Access to entrepreneurial capital

South Sudan has plenty of young entrepreneurs who need capital to fuel their creative business ideas, but the Central Bank has made it difficult for these young people to access financial credit partly because it has never fulfilled its expected role in sufficiently regulating the interest rates. In South Sudan, commercial banks are for-profit companies created to maximize their shareholders' wealth, meaning that they play big and win big when the country's financial regulators are asleep! Since 2005, these banks have made millions of dollars charging borrowers very high-interest rates simply because the watchdog is either dozing off or stagnating in a policy of regulation, particularly of interest rates. How are they supposed to be efficiently regulated and function? To stress this point further, banks are the country's engine of development and growth. They are a catalyst for economic growth and letting them operate as they wish not only hurts entrepreneurs but even the entire economic system. The fake news on social media about a partnership between the

Ministry of Finance and the World Bank to finance entrepreneurs and SMEs was a good lie, which served only to deceive our desperate young people that the government cares about them. It must be understood that news regarding access to capital and the economic performance of financial commodities have a direct impact on the financial markets because the circulation of money often changes at a glance.

The country's economic stakeholders must tread their steps carefully so that young entrepreneurs are saved from this economic desolation or else they will perish in hopelessness. Access to capital is nothing but an important part of starting a business, because you may have a good idea of creating something to add value, to serve the country, or to expand your career, but without capital, no matter how small, you may not be able to implement that idea. Therefore, capital is indispensable, but why is it hard for young entrepreneurs to access it? Why is the central bank so adamant to initiate a system of free rate fix? In other countries where banks are efficiently regulated, the central bank uses the interest rate as a perfect monetary policy tool to accelerate entrepreneurship for young creative minds. In Ethiopia, for example, an investor is properly facilitated through different government-aided platforms to access capital through micro-finance, mini banks, and large commercial banks that make it easier to start one's business even without collateral. You can get a short or medium-term loan using your driving license or a car logbook, and sometimes even without both, just your national ID can serve the purpose. Imagine just how easy that process is and compare it to the current situation in South Sudan where without a land title you can never succeed in securing a loan.

Here, the Central Bank expects young entrepreneurs to find collateral if they are to be given loans and this only hinders their entrepreneurial potential. I encourage commercial banks to be more just and creative in this regard. Bank managers should devise some of the other creative ways of granting the young South Sudanese investors quick business-launch loans without attaching stringent conditions. The bank may simply partner with the young entrepreneurs in areas including business financial management, or enter into a sort of joint venture which can benefit both entities while attracting other youths into entrepreneurship. The government should not sit back and relax while expecting the youths to empower themselves, but rather, through the relevant ministries it can negotiate with commercial banks to enable the young entrepreneurs to access loans at a subsidized rate. Today most commercial banks give loans at interest rates between twenty and thirty-five percent, which I believe is too exploitative. I doubt that foreign banks can charge this much in their home countries, but then, why do they do it here? Simply, it is because our economy is in tatters as the Central Bank is at a trying time and our financial legal framework isn't fulfilling. Therefore, the Central Bank should wake up and rescue our budding entrepreneurs from this shameful exploitation by foreign-owned banks. The government should also collaborate with development partners or agencies to try and ease the cost of doing business, especially for our young people. Without those much-needed policy changes, our financial freedom and economic independence will be wiped away by the new financial mafias and the dignity of our beloved nation will be jeopardized.

Achieving financial freedom

Financial freedom is a state in which the individual can satisfy most, if not all, of his needs at any given time without monetary stress. This is when a person has an abundance of resources, free from debt, and enjoys a greater measure of financial independence. At this level, a person either works to pass on his experience or because he loves the job. People think that financial freedom is difficult to achieve because there are no clear and direct means to become financially free. Though everybody thrives to be financially free, not all become so despite the many attempts. Poverty is evil, and it is the source of most, if not all, bad things that can happen to a person. If you are poor and unable to bring food to the table, you may become agitated by the situation, become overwhelmed by anxiety, commit suicide, or hurting fellow human beings. Think of the lack of everything, from necessities to luxury materials, and tell me if poverty is not the cause. So, it is important to be in a position to at least provide for basic needs like food, clothing, medicals, and security as you cannot live without them, and gradually you can attain financial freedom to live life to the fullest.

I know you are waiting for the answer on how you can free yourself financially, but let me say this to you first: money is unbiased and never discriminates based on one's color, race, tribe, or religion. It avails itself to everyone that works hard for it. It is something to do with your attitude towards money, the way you earn it, spend it, or save it that determines whether you will financially be independent or not. If one learns the rightful methods correctly, then there cannot be bad luck with acquiring money. Remember, I am not talking about corrupt money or cash obtained through shoddy deals. I am an advocate of clean wealth creation. I would like everyone to own a business, no matter how small, as long as you can make a living and earn clean money, that should be the right way to go and to do things. Perhaps you now have an idea of what I am talking about. My readers, please remember that there are no shortcuts to making money if you want to be financially free. I believe that if you follow the following steps, you should be financially independent. In the business world, they say that business is an idea, not capital. The phrase implies that if you have a brilliant idea that can create value for you and for whoever is involved at the end of this deal, then you are a businessman with the potential to create wealth that can go on to create more wealth. Here your proposal is financially promising, and there are many examples of people doing very clean business between Mombasa and Sudan, or Kampala and Juba, without a dent. Just clean-cutting deals.

Therefore, I encourage all young people to adopt the mindset of a hardworking entrepreneur. For starters, an entrepreneur is a person who recognizes a business opportunity, takes risks to invest in, and operates a profit-making venture. An entrepreneur creates wealth through hard work and persistence. The whole world is run by entrepreneurs who work very hard to make the impossible possible and you can become one of them and change your country for the common good. Think of *Bill Gates, Aliko Dangote, Larry Page, Jeff Bezos, Michael Bloomberg, Walt Disney, Steve Jobs*, and so many other exemplary entrepreneurs on whose initiatives much of the world is operating. Entrepreneurs are not only persistent but also risk-taking as they don't mind failing at all. So if you want to be financially free, you need to build this habit of creativity in everything you are involved in. Other entrepreneurial attributes include positive thinking, continuous learning, and excellent leadership in team building. Establish a business network and connect with those who share the same ideas as you, for you can advise and guide each other towards a common goal. Never walk with a fool, or you will be soiled. Collaborate with intelligent ones and those with technical know-how. Don't be overly money-oriented but do business to meet a common good for yourself, family, community, and the nation. Do it because you have identified a problem to solve. Business is done to solve social problems, accelerate life, and advance well-being, not just to accumulate *Gurush (Money)*.

Don't let the lust for quick profits distract you from achieving your business goals. Once you have reached an advanced level of business, you will see how your money works for you while relaxing with your loved ones on the beach of Juba! Believe me, you can build your empire and become your boss. You will master your destiny while working for the government or somebody else. You shouldn't be a salaried employer. Poverty eradication is a collective work, we should not rely on the government to provide us with food. Do you know that the government of the poor is weak? Dr. John Garang once said that if we want to be a rich country, then we should be hard-working citizens because we will pay high taxes and then enrich our government.

If we double our efforts individually to do business while creating wealth, then we can strengthen our government and ultimately become financially free and independent. So the answer to the question of how to be financially free depends on what you do to make money. You can work for the state or private companies and earn a decent salary that in most cases does not meet your needs, enable you to do business, or amass assets, and instead, you will become a passive income earner. Brothers and sisters, have you realized the secret to financial freedom? Entrepreneurship is the only answer to the financial freedom you crave and deserve so much. I guarantee you, if you have valuable assets, you can never do anything wrong.

To move forward and make our economy more competitive in the region, South Sudan needs the innovation, prosperity, and jobs created by our entrepreneurs. We need to have the next *Dangotes* all over the country. The thriving economy is based on a favorable environment for entrepreneurship to flourish and to promote local economic progress, which directly and indirectly employs hundreds of thousands of people. But this ambitious goal can be achieved with the right skills, without which South Sudanese will be unable to reap much for a long time. But, with solid hopes and globalization, young people can hone their entrepreneurial skills if they focus on *Science, Technology, Engineering, and Mathematics (STEM)* and have access to on-job training. This will provide the necessary link between the private sector and the government to strongly promote education and training systems to meet the needs of the country's ever bulging labor market.

Existing companies can get involved in youth empowerment through the provision of apprenticeships, traineeships, and mentorship programs. Our irreversible call for good governance remains intact as we need a government that works hard in providing decent employment opportunities for its competent young people, first by developing a sustainable and diversified national agricultural strategy to achieve food security and stop all the unnecessary food importation. The government must also develop the country's manufacturing system and national value chains by encouraging massive public and private investment in infrastructure development projects that directly and indirectly contribute towards economic and regional integration while also promoting inter-state trade among the South Sudanese. My hope is for an inclusive government that strives to reduce youth unemployment, improve youth productivity, and as young people, we must also get involved by working hand in hand with the public and private sectors to eradicate poverty in South Sudan, through which we can end all the conflicts and other socio-political evils that afflict our beloved nation.

Exclusion from Governance

We have a right to inclusive nation-building

Creating a more inclusive and equitable system of government is not just a prerequisite for the fiduciary relationship between the state and its citizens, but also a precondition for a free, progressive, and democratic society. The concept of fiduciary responsibility imposes positive measures on state-building to protect the economy, physical security, and the well-being of all its people equally, including women and young people. In South Sudan, some citizens are on the fringes of national affairs due to their political loyalty. This is the fate of many communities in the country that may one day support the idea of a federal system that recognizes ethnic and regional diversity. The cardinal authority that guarantees political, social, and economic inclusion is the *Transitional Constitution of the Republic of South Sudan* in which the state is mandated to create an inclusive national system through equitable governance for a harmonious coexistence by both the minority and majority. Appropriate and fair representation takes place when a constituent body is composed of competent delegates from all walks of life representing their various age groups, races, religions, tribes, and genders.

South Sudan has the youngest population in the region, but this young majority is not well represented in either public or private sectors. The gap between the policymakers and the young people creates a huge gap between those in charge and those being controlled, resulting in poor policy and decision-making that never meets people's needs. For decades, even before independence, young people's grievances have largely been ignored by policymakers who think that the youths are neither qualified nor experienced enough to tell them what to do. There is no evidence of the active involvement of young people in state structures or administrative processes. Unfortunately, we are dealing with old leaders and institutions that are unable to take meaningful actions to address the myriad of problems that are critical for the well-being of young people, particularly the lack of access to decent education, unemployment, and the eradication of poverty. If governments instead focused on social inclusion, the youth would have enormous potential to positively impact change and spur economic growth. Senior political leaders - our *Uncles* cruising in V8 Land Cruisers, often view the youths' aspirations as a blend of immorality, cultural invasion, disrespect, and imperialist influences. In any progressive country, youths are the most important economic resource, because not only are they agile, adaptable, and responsive to the ever-changing needs, but the modern youth is also highly informed, competent, and innovative. They are attuned to the opportunities of the gig economy, constantly aware of the latest and newest trends in technology, and ready to take advantage of them at whatever cost or risk.

However, there are some promising ways for promoting the empowerment of young people, especially through employment and the improvement of social welfare for better economic and personal well-being. Above all, we must rethink our education system in South Sudan, where almost all of our universities have been rendered as *"useless"* graduation mills because most of their graduates are unable to provide the much-needed technological and scientific skills that the nation desperately needs to become as advanced as others in the region. These institutions are only good at churning out arts and humanities graduates who are only good at irrelevant classical subjects including history, philosophy, and sociology. Although these are undoubtedly important subjects, we need a complete reinvention of our new education system to train young people to be skilled and technical professionals that can meet the challenges and demands of the 21st century.

We need adequate facilitation of science and technology departments in universities, increase pay for *STEM* instructors, while also encouraging more student enrollment in *STEM* disciplines. Moreover, South Sudan's government must wake up to combat the problem of brain drain because we are losing our highly qualified *STEM* graduates to other countries where their profession is well rewarded. To lure them into staying in South Sudan, we must create favorable conditions, including policy regulation, adequate salaries, and well-equipped facilities, including hospitals, laboratories, and so on. Our young people must be empowered to hold their destiny into their own hands to uplift our nation to scientific and technological supremacy. Today's South Sudanese youths are competently skilled to excel brilliantly in critical areas including leadership and governance, information technology, engineering, peace, and the business sector.

In 2014, I was appointed as the Deputy Chairperson of the *Sudan People's Liberation Movement/Army-in-Opposition (SPLM – IO) Youth League Chapter* in Ethiopia. In this position, I deputized comrade *Riek Zong* who was among the industrious students who campaigned for me to win the seat of the Secretary-General of the *South Sudan University Students' Union in Ethiopia (SSUSUE)*. I didn't campaign for the *SPLM-IO* youth league position as I was endorsed to a higher position of *National Chairperson of the SPLM – IO Youth League* by Hon. Pout Kang Chol, the current Minister of Petroleum in the *RTGoNU*. After our appointment, along with other young volunteers, we willingly performed our duties using our own money, including buying refreshments so that members could feel at home while warming the seats. Some comrades dedicated themselves to the success of the *SPLM-IO Youth League*, although it was only a few of us who struggled to push the group forward.

With Comrade *Riek Zong*, we recruited more youth as we organized more political rallies, some of which were attended by the party chairman. We also organized the *"Red Card"* campaign under the slogan *"Kiir Must Go"*, and many other undertakings to reach-out to more members until I froze my political involvement to focus on my career development as I assumed an important role at the African Union. After my stint with the *SPLM-IO Youth League*, I resolved to become a nation-builder by focusing on youth transformation without any political affiliation despite my membership in the *SPLM-IO*. This experience has led me to define exclusion from two angles; when the young people deliberately distance themselves from politics, and when political leaders do not favor the youth with any governance positions. As the young generation of this country, we must examine the validity of these two realities from different perspectives while considering how we can overcome them to make an active contribution to the development, emancipation, progress, and greatness of South Sudan.

Leadership Without Vision

Without a vision, a nation crumbles...

A simple fact about South Sudan's past and present are the irrelevantly undefined visions that have led us to nowhere. Despite some success stories at the individual level and the triumph of those who believed that independence was essential, South Sudan remains under the custody of visionless leaders for the last nine years which have been characterized by insecurity and unimaginable poverty. There is no evidence of adequate basic public services for ordinary citizens or the implemented government-sponsored projects, except those sponsored and carried out by the various international development agencies operating within South Sudan. Because of our visionless leaders, South Sudanese have suffered enormous challenges due to conflict, the lack of adequate education, and poor economic conditions.

Many of us have sought a modest education in the neighboring countries and have had to endure an unpleasant reputation for which our country is well-known. This stigmatizes us psychologically. The visionless elites have invested heavily in weapons that cause endless political strife, militarizing the nation, promoting tribalism, and spreading dynastic corruption tendencies all of which have created a lustful desire for power as a means for plundering public resources and buying mansions abroad. Such social vices have become the norm in South Sudan's governance system because they are deeply embedded in our state institutions, and are therefore a critical element of the administrative system. The effects are continuous conflicts, the failure to understand people's needs, militarizing the country's politics *(SPLM-In-Charge vs SPLM-In-Opposition)*, thus throwing the country in endless mayhem.

In a country where ethnical conflicts take the center stage, selfish political interests replace national interests as the priority of leaders without a national vision. Their visionless leadership is characterized by the massive plunder of national resources, the appointment of relatives and tribe-mates into public positions, and prioritizing development in particular regions. The question that remains is: *What does the future behold for South Sudan?* During the last decade, there have been no promising signs of a change in the governance norm; it is not even clear how we will achieve sustainable development that could reduce poverty across the country and contribute to achieving the SDGs by 2030. The only achievement of which we can slyly be proud of is the eagerness to steal from the young, inexperienced, and the vulnerable nation - a dream by those with aspirations in the political arena. This is all because we are a country without a laid out strategic vision for pro-people civilian rule.

Since we are stuck with visionless leaders, we now have malfunctioning branches of the government turning into *Executhieves, Legislooters,* and *Judisharing* which have made us become defined as a failed state by global standards. Cartels rule this country and use this state of anarchy to plunge our economy further into the abyss. The vision of the *Oyee Party* died with the founding father of the *SPLM/A*, the late *Dr. John Garang De Mabior*, who championed for the new Sudan while presenting his vision wherever he went, whether in the war jungles or large cities, he simply explained his vision of how Sudan can be transformed. Since his demise, we have lacked someone formidable enough to campaign for a new prosperous and united South Sudan. Since 2005, political uprisings, inconclusive peace talks, conflicts between communities, and armed village youth seeking revenge became the order of the day.

The *SPLM/A* leadership of the time was desperate for South Sudan to become independent, however, they forgot to lay the foundations for the peaceful post-referendum period and the cessation of fighting. There was a vision of New *South Sudan* before the country was left in the hands of political vultures who never thought of developing a strategic vision for national development based on the people's interests and protected by the national virtues. The phenomenon of divide and rule is reaching its peak in all state institutions which are occupied by cartels both within the country and in the diaspora, also visible on social media where hate speech is the main dialect. Youths are the driving force when it comes to spreading tribalistic messages rather than advocating for ideas of transformation, development, and the country's renaissance. The tribal conflict that is prevalent among our visionless current leaders has fostered bloody tensions between our communities while disrupting the social fabric of the people - a phenomenon that many have embraced because of its spread.

We must understand that tribal affiliation is itself not an obstacle to lasting peace, but the wicked negative minds that cause all conflicts and wars that plague our country. This is a question of individual mentality - one that accepts corruption, greed, pride, and a lack of patriotism. Tribalists hate harmonious coexistence between different communities and work untiringly to destabilize even the slightest cordial relation between different tribes. There is a strong need for eradicating such negative attitudes, whether educated or ignorant, the character remains the same, but those who have acquired formal education are the worst tribal disciples. The youth should embrace exemplary leadership akin to the biblical Joseph and Prophet Daniel who were responsible servants with dignity in serving God and the people of Israel. We are in the *Promised Land*, in an independent South Sudan, but to achieve the life we always dream of, we must adopt a strategically beneficial vision for the current and future generations. It remains important to rejuvenate our mindset to create a righteous generation with a common goal, dream, and vision for a prominent South Sudan that we all want - a country that can be proud of the generous contributions of its youth.

The lack of intergenerational dialogue exacerbated the conflicts in the new nation of South Sudan, and when intergenerational cooperation became obsolete, people simply acted decisively without wasting a single thought even when this meant the destruction and the loss of many lives. As a failed state, we suffer immensely from the misdeeds of the *SPLM/A*'s *dinosaur* generation of 1983, which failed to emulate the visionary 1956 revolutionaries. They have turned our country upside down as it has become a shadow of its former self whose leaders laid down their lives for nation-building. Now we have the inexperienced millennials lusting to replace the aging *Uncles* and inherit their scandalous leadership styles. Now is the right time to formulate the *South Sudan Vision 2035* before things get out of hand.

South Sudan Vision 2035

South Sudan Vision 2035 is a vision by a young man in his late twenties in which he explains the possible solutions to the sustainable development and nation-building challenges in the next fifteen years. This vision is by someone who was born and raised amidst the proliferating conflicts and wars of that time. It is based on the theme of achieving real freedom, equality, fairness, harmony, and prosperity for all. The vision builds on the country's strengths and opportunities, including the full exploitation of its rich natural resources while encouraging the skilled young people to face the challenges of building a strong nation by fighting poverty, improving the Human Development Index, and creating sustainable peace and security for all.

The vision is rooted in a carefully prepared analysis of three key aspects of the South Sudan context: *conflict, poverty,* and *macroeconomics*. Among the objectives of a new nation recovering from conflict and wishing to progress onto a fast-track development path, security is a priority because the very lack of it becomes a blockade to national development. Examples include the 2013 - 2020 war that followed the *SPLM/A* House's downfall, the inter-communal clashes between tribes over cattle and access to grazing land, the breakdown of cultural values and norms, arms proliferation, and the absence of economic opportunities. We are now a country where citizens displace their fellow citizens, persistent food insecurity is the order of the day, incompetent leadership is the norm, poor service delivery is the character, and widespread levels of poverty is our identity. The following are the key reform points in the South Sudan Vision 2035:

★ **Poverty eradication**

Poverty eradication requires an exceptional focus on rural transformation and the provision of basic social services through the extension of agricultural resources, health and sanitation facilities, good schools, technology, and industrialization. Rural development will be crucial in particular to improving livelihoods, food security, and increasing employment opportunities for the very large number of poor people in slums, and rural communities across the country, especially women and the young people. This will require continued improvements in transport infrastructure, increased agricultural and livestock productivity, solving of land wrangles, and improving access to ready markets, agricultural inputs, micro-finance, and agricultural extension services. Rural development measures also help to diversify the economy.

Leadership Without Vision

★ **Inclusive security**

Improved security and lasting peace undoubtedly bring about a sense of belonging brought about by the secure environment of doing business and enjoying the freedom of the land. Security is important for the business environment to thrive and build trust in the country's governance structures which are key in attracting both local, regional, and international investors. Clarifying issues of grazing and land rights is important to prevent further conflict and is part of the basis for much-needed rural development. The new nation must implement and consolidate the gains from the institutional and governance mechanisms developed during the entirety of the *RTGoNU*. Good governance, including transparency and accountability, creates confidence, fosters stability while improving credibility in the government. To ensure that South Sudan is a united and peaceful new nation by 2035, we must lay a strong foundation for good governance, economic prosperity, and improved quality of life for all South Sudanese.

★ **Good governance**

As the country emerges from the ashes of its devastating and sharply divisive civil wars, adopting good governance and improving capacity is crucial to restoring the lost credibility and effectiveness of medium to long-term development efforts by the government. The Government must be committed to ensuring an independent and effective Legislature which can hold the Executive to account, and an independent judiciary that upholds the rule of law while protecting the rights of all its citizens. Members of the Legislature must be duly elected by people from their respective local constituencies instead of the current hand-picked political appointees who swap the nation's priorities to worship of the master.

★ **Social inclusion**

The Government should focus on addressing any potential conflicts and challenges by being as open, welcoming, and inclusive as possible. The drafting process for the permanent constitution and the constitutional conference should be transparent through open and broad participation from all over the country. There must be a balanced involvement of different groups in governance and public administration, including gender diversity in public institutions, the consideration of public input in the country's policy and decision-making, with no less than fifty percent of all administrative posts being occupied by women, while the youth should be represented by not less than thirty-five percent.

★ **Accountability and transparency**

The country's public audit systems must be strengthened, timely audit processes established, and reports shall be forwarded to the parliament for further scrutiny and then released to the public. Furthermore, actions to strengthen the capacity of the parliament in its oversight functions must be carried out. All public office holders shall be obliged to declare their assets or wealth before and after assuming the public service positions from the junior to the highest-ranking government officials.

★ **Civil service improvement**

The public service recruitment system needs to be revised to ensure that it fully meets both the government and the public's needs. As well, a performance management system needs to be introduced to check on the best and worst-performing departments. Meanwhile, vigorous training efforts shall resume enhancing professionalism in public service delivery.

★ **Economic growth**

Sustainable economic growth and development led by a burgeoning private sector will be crucial for South Sudan's future prosperity and for defusing the potentiality of conflicts. For national development to be pro-poor, it must both be diversified and equitable. The initial emphasis shall be on using money from oil exportation to drive rural economic recovery and development as envisioned by *Dr. John Garang*. The economy needs to diversify to create much-needed employment to improve livelihoods, especially for former combatants who are not only important in the fight against poverty but also central towards maintaining peace and security among their peers and communities.

★ Infrastructural development

This involves the development and modernization of transport infrastructure to meet international standards and local needs. Better roads help rural farmers to easily transport their produce to the markets without compromising the quality of their products. Major roads that link Juba to other strategic towns must be upgraded to the tarmac, feeder roads must be leveled, and their regular maintenance is prioritized. Noteworthy examples include the *Juba-Bor* and the *Juba-Rumbek* whose completion must be pushed on.

★ Access to financial services

We need to open up all financial and credit services to become accessible to all people regardless of their background. There is a strong need for introducing financial regulation laws to protect the business environment and the country's economic interests. This will go a long way towards resolving issues related to financial misappropriation while also bringing essential financial services closer to the people wherever they happen to be.

★ Access to social services

Improving access to social services is a key priority for action in the context of social and human development. Concerning the health sector, the government should work with other social care providers to improve equitable access to quality basic social services throughout the country including health care, education, subsidized housing, the extension of electricity and clean water, security, and community management. Among the core health sector objectives, there must be the elimination of all maternal and infant mortality rates, regular vaccinations, and a comprehensive training program for health professionals. There must also be measures to improve the pharmaceutical and medical equipment supply chains.

★ Education for all

In the field of education, measures should aim to ensure fair participation in a rapidly expanding and high-quality education system. Specific educational objectives include increasing the *Net Enrolment (NET)* rate for primary schools, doubling the *NET* for secondary schools, and reducing the ratio between qualified teachers and pupils. Key actions include: (a) accelerating intensive teacher training, (b) accelerating the investment programs for building and refurbishing learning centers and facilities, and (c) developing and implementing strategies for keeping the girl-child in school, including the provision of school meals, upgrading facilities, and expanding community and secondary schools for girls, and the disabled. From a quality perspective, we should also focus on improving teacher motivation and professional education development, disseminating the national curriculum for primary and secondary schools, and making textbooks and computers available.

★ Conflict prevention

This presents a daunting dilemma. National security takes up a significant portion of the national budget which leaves other key sectors with insufficient funds for development and growth. Efforts to increase security and deepen the peace-building structures must focus on consolidating lasting peace among the warring communities. All persistent and deep-rooted sources of internal conflict will be solved through comprehensive national and local peace dialogue and reconciliation programs. Specifically, there will be a comprehensive national program to transform the uniformed security services to become the people's security forces - one that also addresses demobilization needs holistically, including *Disarmament, Demobilization, and Reintegration (DDR)* while providing incentives to all ex-combatants.

★ Access to justice

This will ensure a well-functioning criminal justice system irretrievably linked to peace-building and the provision of alternative options for resolving disputes without recourse to conflicts. There will be a strengthened criminal justice system that respects everyone's human rights while applying the legal framework to give due justice to all. Police community relations committees will be established at the county level and community security approaches will be introduced in all ten states. Besides, the systems for conflict mediation and reconciliation will be developed further to suit all the involved parties' interests and meet their needs.

★ **Monitoring and evaluation**

This includes a systemic framework to track how much has been spent and what has been achieved with all public spending to achieve the social and economic development priorities of the nation. The framework will examine the achievements to determine whether the intended objectives were achieved, and where necessary, changes will be made in public procurement and other public dealings. Monitoring will recommend adjustments to be made where necessary, especially when particular programs, outputs, and activities are no longer considered effective or when changes are required to implement the strategy in the medium term.

Humble Beginnings

Success requires perseverance and hard work

There is nothing more rewarding in life than a humble beginning. It all starts with a simple act of volunteering and community service which prepares the individual to acquire relevant humanitarian skills, accumulate knowledge while developing a spirit of social belonging. Our country is filled with so much pain and misery that sometimes I fear for the vulnerable youths who lack the skills to navigate their way through the challenges and achieve their goals and dreams of both individual and national development. The years of conflict may have severed all social ties, but I remain firmly convinced that we will do a splendid job of transforming and developing South Sudan. I am optimistic that the youth of this country, when they one day take over the administration of our country, will do exceptionally well, much better than any previous government.

To help you better navigate the narrow, straight, and crooked paths you may encounter, in this section, I am sharing with you one valuable lesson from my life experiences as I contributed towards peace-building in the motherland. Never despise humble beginnings, there is a reason why it is called the start because it is the very commencement of something, and the start can be challenging and difficult. This is why some give up so easily and so early but the more patience, commitment, concentration, openness to service, and humility you demonstrate, the easier it will be. Remember that the first cut is the deepest.

I have enjoyed unique opportunities to connect and mentor many promising young people across the continent, but as I have noted, some of you want to succeed almost immediately as soon as you start. Many of you have a tremendous intolerance for a humble start, and hence, you compromise yourself by engaging in various illegal activities and social vices so you can shine and glitter fast. Remember also that a baby cannot sit up, crawl, walk, or run at the moment of birth as this takes weeks, months, and years of trying. A lot of our young people today want to be born and run the

Humble Beginnings

following day. Take volunteering, for example, which most young people today do not understand. Throughout South Sudan, there are many complaints of unemployment due to various well-known reasons and other factors. However, not many are willing to volunteer without compensation and financial support.

In 2017, I worked for a year as a volunteer for the UNHCR Ethiopia, it was tough, but I persisted because I had a burning desire to serve humanity, especially working with displaced people and refugees from different countries. Later, in 2018, I was offered a paid position with the *Jesuit Refugee Service (JRS)*, an implementation partner of the UNHCR, which deals with child protection and the provision of urban services to, particularly vulnerable refugees. I agreed to work as a *Refugee Outreach Volunteer (ROV)* to gain life experiences that cannot be equated with a college degree. Young people should consider ways of gaining hands-on work experience in the field even during their studies because most feel entitled to work for only a few months and then demand hefty compensation worth years of work. Other factors that hinder young people's professional growth include an insatiable lust for materialism as there is a huge appetite for material wealth immediately after school or college. As soon as they graduate, young people are increasingly engaging in illicit ways of getting expensive stuff like cars, jewelry, women, and mansions.

Don't get me wrong: I am all for ambitious young people striving for a better life and an eminent career. However, such ambitious pursuits must always be accompanied by patience and perseverance. Every life that is in the fast lane is a life that will soon get out of hand - except that life that goes through many chapters to learn and experience. Consider your early beginning as a roadmap for where you want to go and how you want to proceed. You cannot begin and end your life in the first chapter. Write your pages slowly but carefully, focus on the goals you have set for yourself, and stick to God. You will soon discover that humbleness is an outstanding type of beginning. Be patient and listen. These two characters will make you unconquerable and ready to start from the bottom and up until you reach the mountaintop. If one listens to his heart, then there is time to discover the purpose of his existence and to concentrate on the progressive development that will attract loyal people, work with reputable organizations, companies, and philanthropies that seek to better the lives of others.

My Journey from the Land of Great Abundance to the African Union

Currently, I am a *Youth Volunteer* with the *African Union (AU)* attached to the *Department of Trade and Industry*, specifically working as a *Mining Policy Officer*. My journey goes back to 2012, the first leg to Addis Ababa the new flower and the headquarters of the African Union whose aim is to advance Africa's rapid integration and sustainable development. The AU is doing this by promoting unity, solidarity, cohesion, and cooperation among the peoples of Africa and by developing a new partnership at the global level. Its mission is to achieve the Africa we want, as enshrined in *Agenda 2063*, Africa's *Sustainable Development Goals (SDGs)* initiative for the next 43 years. Venturing into the African Union was by no means easy as I had no insider connections, neither relatives nor friends working for the *African Union Commission (AUC)* to approach for guidance into the magnificent building. Although I was content with a simple stroll through the grounds, deep inside, I longed to explore what the African Union was doing to realize a prosperous and peaceful continent. That was in March 2012, barely a month after the *Head of States and Governments' annual Summit (HoSG)* where African Presidents converged in the building to discuss policies, burning agendas, treaties, and partnerships relating to Africa.

I immediately decided to enter the building to experience it for myself and learn about the African Union. I went in with less hope, presuming that I would be denied access by the guards guarding the entrance, much like the UN security personnel. Surprisingly, I found out, it was easy! I simply used my blue ordinary passport to enter the complex as a guest. By then, entrance by the Access Code was not yet introduced and the *'China Building' (the new AU building)* had just been inaugurated. Once there, I visited the *Mwalimu Nyerere Peace and Security Complex, the Nelson Mandela Conference Hall*, and thereafter had a short walk to marvel at some iconic historical portraits. At first, it was not a pleasant experience, so I rushed out and picked up my passport, and headed home. Later that night I wondered if I had learned anything new from my visit that day. I answered myself with a bold NO! Out of curiosity, I browsed the official website of the African Union to learn more about the activities and functions of the organization. Then I learned about its administrative structures, goals, mission, and vision. Finally, I came across the 'Job Section' for those willing to join the AU workforce. I checked to seek opportunities for vacancies, internships, and

Humble Beginnings

volunteering. By then, I had recently dropped out of the University of Al-Neelain in Sudan *(due to South Sudan's secession from united Sudan in 2011)*.

Joining the AU was not in my vocabulary at the time but I was eager to learn more about the union's activities. I had read extensively about the continent's holistic progressive *Agenda 2063* in the making, yet, I had no idea of getting involved in its actualization. Later on, I learned about a *Youth Division* under the *Human Resources Sciences and Technology (HRST)* department. It is currently led by *H.E. Prof. Sarah Anyang Agbor* the iron lady who champions the empowerment of the young people and always encourages the African youth to become a proactive generation. Her famous quote is: *"If you think you can't change anything, then you have never spent the night with a mosquito."* Thus, she appreciates our collective unwavering call for the transformation and development of the continent by the youth. This includes the *Africa We Want* initiative which aims at realizing the full potential of the women and the young people while caring for the children to promote prosperous Africa.

I was inclined to read more about the *African Youth Charter*, the *AU Development Framework*, and *Pan-Africanism* - the values that I am solemnly prepared to impart to everyone on the continent in my capacity as a volunteer with the African Union. Talking of the *African Union Youth Volunteer (AUYVC)* program, it allows young African professionals within and in the diaspora to contribute their quota to the development of the continent. The *Ubuntu Champions (youth volunteers)* are trained and recruited to work for 12 months in African Union member states other than their own. It is a very competitive program for all young people wishing to join the African Union who have at least one year of experience in volunteering in a recognized organization.

Other criteria include having at least two years of professional experience, between the ages of 18 and 35, being a national of a member state residing anywhere in the world, and willing to serve the continent. Believe me, you do not need insider connections to join the African Union. Only your competence and passion will get you where you want to serve. I applied for the AUYVC program for the first time in 2014 but I was not successful. In 2016 and 2018 I tried again with a similar fate. Then I filled the online application again in June 2019, giving my experience in volunteering with *UNHCR Ethiopia*, the *Jesuit Refugee Service*, and my experience in mining. Yes, I was a refugee who enjoyed serving other refugees, and the few contributions that I made in teaching language classes and in translating documents proved so valuable as I diligently served humanity.

I was shortlisted in September 2019 for a two-week preparatory training in December 2019 in Cairo, Egypt. During the training, we got acquainted with the *Pan Africanism Ideology, Afro-Centricity, Black Consciousness, African Feminism, Liberating African Culture, Land Sovereignty, Youth Development, Empowerment, Gender Mainstreaming, a.k.a Gender-Box, Tubonge Episodes*, and our roles as *AUYVCs*. Although I missed my AU sponsored flight from Addis Ababa to Cairo, I had to book a new ticket. I took the night flight with EgyptAir the following day and made it to Cairo at 02:00 without anyone at the airport to pick me up. Fortunately, I spoke fluent Arabic and it was my fourth visit to Egypt, so I ordered an Uber taxi to take me to the TOLIP Inn El Maadi. I enjoyed my 12 days of engagement with professionals from the African Union and other trainers from *Ecobank* and the *Center for Youth Development Services (C4YDS)*. After graduation, I received an invitation to attend the *World Youth Forum 2019* in Sharm el Sheik as a Speaker on the topic: *The Role of Civil Society Organizations in Post-Conflict Reconstruction and Development in Africa*. It was another fantastic experience to interact in an environment of around 7,000 participants from all walks of life - such an exciting experience!

Afterward, I was notified of a deployment offer in January 2020, while it took six months to be recruited at the *Department of Trade and Industry of the African Union Commission* in Addis Ababa. The delay was not due to the Covid-19 but to the normal AU bureaucracy in recruitment. The Covid-19 pandemic forced authorities around the world to take preventive measures, including lockdowns of varying severity such as border closures, school closures, jobs, and limiting large public gatherings. The situation affected the African Union's operations, as *working from home* became the new reality. Recently, in May 2020, the first virtual onboarding for the young volunteers was introduced and several of my colleagues from the *10th Nile AUYVC* group were deployed. I developed a strong interest in resuming my engagement by highlighting the situation in South Sudan and exposing the misconceptions of violence and conflict for which the country is known due to the lack of lasting peace and stability. Deep in my heart, South Sudan is still a country of a million hopes – *The Land of Great Abundance and the Eden of Diversity*.

One particular problem that I would like to raise about my country is the poor internet access and connection which are all prohibitive because they make the internet to be much more expensive in comparison to other African countries. Internet service providers *(MTN and Zain)* charge $800 for broadband installation plus a $300 monthly fee. Still, you have to struggle with the low speeds to conduct or join a Zoom meeting. Despite the setbacks, I try to network and do my job on time whatever the cost. This is the most important challenge of the new decade - to close the ever-widening gap in the digitally divided world. I started my virtual engagement smoothly, but other challenges remain, especially when you need to be in a quiet place with a stable connection and avoid distractions like pushy family members who think that you are talking to your girlfriend or chatting to friends. But I keep telling them that I have a serious business meeting at a certain time and that I would prefer to be left alone for more concentration and focus. In general, this is the new norm, as my working life with *Zoom, Microsoft Teams, Bluejeans,* and *Cisco WebEx* teams is conducted while maintaining data security practices; the new reality imposed on us by Covid-19.

I dedicate this section to all the able young Africans who want to learn more about the *AUYVC* program and to those who wish to contribute to the desired changes on the continent in all circumstances. The truth is that you can contribute to the *Africa We Want*, even if you are not officially part of the African Union. It remains our individual and collective effort as a promising young generation to give a valuable meaning to volunteering while improving the livelihoods of our communities across the continent. Therefore, if you find an opportunity to join the African Union, you will go through the same process as I did, and you will ultimately be there to mark your lasting contribution and commitment to the achievement of a prosperous, peaceful, and an integrated Africa that we all want, wish for, hope for, and treasure.

Perfecting the Storm

We will rise...after the dark storms

F aced with worsening economic crisis, hunger, COVID-19, and the relentless conflicts in all walks of life, many of us tend to lose the drive to carry on after realizing that our children have little to eat and are therefore unable to meet their basic needs. We compare ourselves with others and feel that nothing will work in this rapidly changing world. For others who are rejected, endure the pain and hardships, it appears that the gates of heaven should simply open before them so that they may find peace with God because they are tired of the earthly life which is like a punishment to them. Everything we fight for, hoping to make the best of it, ends in grief and sorrow. The problematic situation makes us feel completely rejected and abandoned by the creator of the universe. But for me, I think otherwise as I had my worries and desires simultaneously but I didn't let the negativities sink in.

Going through difficulties does not mean that you will never overcome such worries while climbing the mountain of life. I have the feeling that we should all struggle with life for all the days that God gives us. It is not easy to wrestle something that is so wearisome to confront or grasp, but that is the only way out. Life is a series of painful events some of which make us cry as they deprive us of hope, but conversely, they make us strong. We have to accept the fact that life is unfair, and that is a miserable reality for all of us when we sleep too much. We will only wake up to realize it is another brand-new day, and that the whole world has moved on while you were deeply asleep. Life may be too hard for you, but you have not yet listened to other people's complicated life stories, and if someone opens up to you regarding their struggles, you will then stop complaining and just thank God for your less-weighty situation. Life is hard for many in South Sudan, including the young generations *(the Millennial and Z Generation)*, and something must be done to change this.

We cannot think of demanding our rights like dragging a sheep into a slaughterhouse by giving in to the broken system. We must fight for what is, of course, naturally ours, to live a free life, for which our independence fighters fought. But amid the storms of violence and failed governance, there is still a glimmer of hope. Anything wrong in our country can be reformed by working hand-in-hand with all the concerned policymakers, including those in the legislature, executive, and judiciary to implement the much-needed reforms for developing our nation. We can also work with the private and business sectors, development partners including OXFAM, World Vision, the United Nations, and others to promote peace, social inclusion, and opportunities for creativity and youth employment. Such influential but neutral policymakers, with wholesome intentions for our country, can be our strategic pro-people allies when it comes to influencing policy changes and representing the voice of the ordinary people.

Historically, the most successful social movements have comprised coalitions between the primary mobilization of constituents *(the mass mobilization of people to pursue their rights and interests)* and the secondary activism of professionals who can use the tools of public opinion, law, and international alliances to lead such movements. Principled activism by lawmakers and judges is also crucial, however, there have been few successful primary-secondary coalitions on our continent. The nonviolent independence movement of the 1950s and 1960s was a case in point as the anti-apartheid movement was a variant on the theme. The short-lived civil coalition that overthrew the Nimeiri dictatorship in Sudan in April 1985 was another, and subsequently, the civil uprise that led to the downfall of the *National Congress Party's (NCP)* government which saw the former president *Omar al Bashir* placed behind bars to face crimes relating to abuse of office for more than 30 years.

The pro-democracy movements of the late 1980s and the sovereign national conferences of Francophone countries in early 1990 were other encouraging cases. For many reasons, peace movements are easy to divide or manipulate, and it takes remarkably courageous individuals to resist the taunts of a traitor razed to the ground by one side or the other. In attempting to explain the insufficient social mobilization in South Sudan, we must turn our attention to the reigning political environment. There are many dimensions to this, including the extent to which the society is organized based on citizenship or kinship, the extent of economic development and, in particular, industrialization, and the character of politics, in particular, the extent of militaristic governance. This discussion aims only to isolate one of these dimensions as it proposes a simple four-fold categorization of all kinds of political authority in South Sudan. The categorization applies in various forms both to governments and rebel movements and to the systems of left and right rule.

Whether civil war or interstate war, a tolerant liberal government, when in war mode, will tend to destroy or distort the systems of political representation. Suddenly, dissent can be considered treason or worse. Rebel groups and militias usually rely on the total loyalty of their subjects for their political survival. War does not mean, however, that there is no channel of communication, no possibilities of organization and expression. The following categorization ranges from collapsed states to liberal democracies - just in this case, the narrative of what type of civil society is possible and what it can do. Note that in this context civil society comprises the civilian political parties, trade unions, and other organized interest groups, as well as NGOs and community-based organizations.

Category one consists of the collapsed or failed states characterized by the ineffective governing authority, including the disorganized administration by the militia groups or former rebel fronts. The possibility for any former civilian mobilization is minimal and will probably be limited to local NGOs striving to protect and help the displaced, perhaps with the help of international donors. However, organized political representation is impossible. This draws attention to the fact that in most situations of armed conflict, the primary need for each individual is security and survival, yet, these needs are best met by seeking the protection of a party to the conflict which in turn implies remaining loyal without ever challenging that party's leadership, principles, and ideologies.

Where the conflict has a regional or ethnic dimension, these loyalties can become by far the most important organizing principle so that individuals are not interested in defending their interests as women, youth, and the poor but instead identify with the political and military struggles. Those who resist this identification may be branded as traitors and hence crushed. However, we must not include all countries affected by the conflict in this group, which implies that nothing can be done. This is for a reason that such countries at war could still engage in one way or another in civilian politics after embracing peace and development. For example, Sudan had a functioning parliamentary system between 1986 and 1989 despite being at war. Even in the war-ravaged D.R Congo, the city of Kinshasa still enjoys civil space and political activities of all sorts.

Second, the warring parties themselves are very different in their internal organization, because while some are highly authoritarian and may even be within the personal power sphere of their leaders, others have the capacity for civil administration and the implementation of social programs that can promote the emancipation of marginalized groups such as women. Moreover, in some countries with collapsed states, some areas may be peaceful because they are well facilitated by grassroots administrations and civil society organizations with generous funding from international development partners. This is the case in many parts of Somalia. In other cases, however, the social order is so widespread that any form of organized representation of interest groups is impossible.

Category two is the personal or arbitrary rule manifested in some governments and many armed groups. Policies are inconsistent as political activity is focused on taking or retaining power and enriching the already powerful. A disadvantaged group, including women and the poor, has no political voice, and effective public action on their behalf is unlikely and when it does occur, it is unlikely to last long due to misplaced priorities. Remember that if these groups dare to question the authority of the government, they will be crushed with full force. Even raising alternative agendas and viewpoints can be politically and personally dangerous.

In Africa, most such systems of government are dominated by a masterly man trying to conjure up traditional conceptualizations of the nation's father or tribal leader. Its citizens are infantilized as subjects who should be grateful for their leader's generosity and consideration, hence they are made too powerless to demand their rights. The egotistical man does not consult as he only preaches. In rural areas where adapted traditional forms of authority prevail, this type of rule tends to be much more effective than in urban areas. Any civilized society will therefore be largely an urban phenomenon, born of the same social groups that mobilize opposition political parties and demand greater political freedoms. The government will always tend to dismiss both civil society leaders and opposition politicians as selfish elites.

Options and Strategies for Civil Society

The above categorization underscores how difficult it is inherently for civil society groups to mobilize the masses when they need them most. It emphasizes how the interests of stakeholders can be linked primarily to ethnic, regional, or political affiliations on which survival and security depend in the short term while drawing attention to the strategies that such groups are likely to pursue. During the conflict, the primary identity of a civil society organization of the social group based on ethnic, religious, political, and regional affiliation and the need for physical security always coincide with the main agenda of one of the parties in the conflict.

Only when political tensions ease, for example, in the context of hopeful peace negotiations, will it become possible to mobilize cross-party loyalties, implying that civil society can mobilize for peace only if it is already on the agenda of the main warring parties. A variant of this occurs when a group can work within the institutions established by one of the parties and attempt to test the autonomy of that institution. Another variant occurs when an independent group shows solidarity with one of the parties and attempts to pursue a background agenda that promotes the rights of certain interest groups. In this way, a women's organization can aim to promote women's rights within a particular party or territory it controls.

All groups will be punctilious in performing any visible mobilization in a way that challenges the warring party under whose authority or jurisdiction they operate. A group with an existing constituency in the region - for example, a church organization - will be vigilant to protect its constituents' interests by trying not to offend the party in control. But, under certain circumstances, it may be willing to stand up boldly and publicly for its interests, confident that its combination of local constituencies and international connections will provide some protection. Groups can use external links with international NGOs and exile groups to promote their particular interest and viewpoint or to create a space where broader issues including peace can be discussed. Rapid change is still much needed in South Sudan, either through complete change through a revolution or an amendment to the transitional constitutions in place since 2005. In political science, a revolution is a fundamental and relatively sudden change in political power and administration that occurs when the population revolts against the sitting government, typically due to perceived oppression *(political, social, economic)* or political incompetence. Revolutions should not always be violent, but only seek to establish a new and correct political system that works for everyone in society. Given our militarized mindset that believes nothing will work without guns, we must encourage the adoption of sweeping changes in all social structures, economic, and political institutions.

Is Arab Spring the Perfect Storm?

The notion of a rising tide of young people thirsting for democracy, human rights, and the rule of law is further challenged by the fact that political outcomes in terms of democratic governance to protect the rights of individuals are not what first comes to mind for the majority who have been surveyed. In the *Arab Transformations Survey*, respondents were asked which two factors were most influential in their country for bringing protesters to the streets in or around 2011. There were variations by country, but only minor and sporadic differences between generations, with young people citing one factor more often in one country and the oldest less so in another. More than half of those surveyed cited the economic mismanagement, inefficiency in the delivery of basic public services, and corruption in their respective governments as major problems for their revolution.

Autocracy and demands for political freedom were cited by around 20%, as there was no consistent difference between the age groups. To sum it up, the complete picture of young people's engagement in the uprisings is more complex than is often suggested. The age group that is most likely to participate in and adopt a resistance attitude varies from country to country. Some are aged between 18-24, others are between 25-34, while sometimes all those under 45. In some countries, and considering some aspects of the analysis, the age gap does not vary at all except among those aged over 55. Since young people are only a segment of the population, most participants/supporters come from older age groups, although they are less dramatically over-represented.

Indeed, political change was sought, with two regimes overthrown and replaced by electoral democracies *(Egypt and Tunisia)*, a third regime was overthrown and the aftermath was complete chaos as the country plunged into a never-ending state of anarchy *(Libya)*, while two others had to buy themselves out of instability through concessions and subsidies *(Jordan and Morocco)*. However, that was not the only or even the main driving force. Ask people about the main drivers of the uprisings *(or the challenges they face today)* and they are most likely to cite the direct economic factors *(economic depression, lack of jobs, lack of access to basic resources including food, or socially important factors like education and health care)* as well as incompetent leadership, and unfair political representation. Where democracy is called for, it is then made clear that not only is the thin formality of replacing the government with free and fair elections wanted or even the right to criticize the government without fear of reprisals, but also the decent working conditions and kind of life enjoyed by the democracies on the northern side of the Mediterranean. The decision as to what kind of perfect storm that can usher in a prosperous and peaceful country is left to the people of South Sudan.

Ubuntu and Reconciliation

I am because you are...

The truth must be known that we are the most tribalistic people on the face of the earth. Tribalism is a repugnant behavior that endangers our coexistence and harmony. If your understanding of tribalism emanates from what the media tells you, then you are part of the problem. Again, if you have not tried to understand our common history, you are also part of the problem. Those who do not actively promote progress and lasting peace in South Sudan indirectly hinder progress towards sustainable development. If you are sympathetic to tribalism, then you are complicit in all tribalistic social evils that afflict this country.

Injustice against one tribe is an injustice against the entire human race in the new nation. Consider this phrase that embodies the Ubuntu spirit which originated from South Africa: *"There is no me without you and there is no you without me."* Another one goes: *"I am because you are!"*. When it comes to the issues that concern us all, including wars and conflicts, there is nothing like a vote of abstention and the configuration of souls into a tribeless mode. Whether we recognize it or not, everyday we all vote on issues of national security, community conflicts, tribalism, violence, corruption, injustice, poverty, immorality, and the like. Do not sit on the sidelines, do not be passive, but rather, be active and promote our common social well-being as a united people and a nation of South Sudan.

As for the spirit of Ubuntu, I understand that you may be an innocent person because you have always been good to everyone regardless and that there is not a single moment in your life when you pretended to be someone you are truly not. You have always been a strong supporter of a united South Sudan in every situation, but why things are still not working out on your part remains one of the most difficult questions you cannot easily answer. You may have lost someone so dear to you this year alone to unknown gunmen, rebels, military or state security apparatuses. Perhaps you have done your best in agitating for a fair and just South Sudan but have along the way been distracted by the daily problems squinting at you every morning. You may wonder why you are experiencing these problems and why do you have to bear all these challenges! But the answer lies in rock-solid persistence, coherence, and a sustained fighting spirit for what you believe is right for yourself and for our nation to move forward.

Indeed, life will sometimes disappoint us by raising all kinds of problems and we may therefore tend to give up the struggle. In your heart, you are worried about the future of South Sudan, because all the things you have tried have not produced the expected individual and national results. It takes you from pain to pain and the weight hurts carrying for many years. You can't even stretch yourself, the little energy you have is not what it once was when you started mobilizing for national reconciliation and healing. All the wasted energy and in the end achieved nothing. It is truly sad to think of all the people who have had to endure the brunt of being abandoned and those who suffer all sorts of unimaginable atrocities due to the hatred generated by tribalism. But trust me, you are not the only one; many are in a similar situation like you and are asking countless questions, but the country's leaders remain unemotional.

As a young activist, you have come a very long way, but nothing has happened because everything works the other way around, maybe you have been at school all those years and now you are facing an uncertain future without work. Your parents or the community expect you to return what was invested in you while you were studying. You feel like giving up and something in your mind is sounding the alarm that you are living for nothing and this, like the rest of the problems, will force you to your knees to pray. The situation may seem worse to keep you wondering why things always go wrong. You will keep asking until you reach out and seek advice from those who have experienced a similar scenario.

Jesus Christ, by comparison, experienced even worse scenarios. Sometimes it is hard to know the value of these tears, but Jesus Christ shed many more tears than those we shed every day. Jesus became a refugee, was rejected by his people, and on top of that, he starved for more than a month. Above all, he stood out as the greatest man who ever lived. Although he is the Savior and the Redeemer, the context of Jesus' suffering may seem similar to yours. The lesson is that human life changes from evil to good, and it does not matter how long it takes, because the fact remains that while you are still alive, you have an inspiring story to tell. The story of Jesus should and must give us hope and assurance for the eternal life that awaits us, even if you suffer on earth, God will offer you a restful abode in the next eternal life.

Believe me, you have not lost everything, you are a work in progress. These pushbacks and trials will help you to shape your life in the right way. Imagine if your life was easy as you always wished, would you still feel that there is something else you are living for? I don't think so, but I do know that life must be hard and painful to the extent of resorting to suicide as the only way out. Because when things are not so simple, we must work hard while doing our best to live a satisfying and desirable life and motivate ourselves to achieve our goals. There is no sure way to fulfill God's call for us in this world without first facing these challenges, for we must always be ready to bear these earthly burdens, as we still believe that our God will give us the strength to bear them. What we should know is that there is always a good reason for all the bad things happening in our lives. Some shape us, while others show us the right way to turn. So no matter what kind of situation you may find yourself in, just know that God holds the keys to the locks, and he will unlock them safely along the way. By putting God first in all our endeavors for a peaceful nation, let us promote the reconciliation and national healing in South Sudan that we all want to achieve.

Reconciliation and community harmony are the essential features of South Sudan's customary law, with an emphasis on maintaining the balance between family unity and community. These priorities often come at the expense of the protection of individuals or the provision of mechanisms for punishment or redress. Conflict tends to recur when efforts to heal broken societies are not heeded. When there is no news of attempts to resolve conflicts, fatalism intensifies to stir up nervousness, anxiety, and fear in the population which all encourages more violence as people pick up arms to fight and defend themselves against the perceived threats.

It is the responsibility of every individual in the new nation to work towards eternal reconciliation and healing guided by the spirit of Ubuntu. We can all learn a lot from this beautiful philosophy of southern Africa. Ubuntu is essentially about togetherness and how all our actions affect others and society at large; it is a motivation for everyone to live for each other, anywhere. And to understand that, we must realize that we are all connected in a way that can be invisible to the eye; that there is unity with humanity, and that we lift ourselves by sharing with others and caring for our fellow human beings. Ubuntu speaks of the fact that we are all interconnected and that you can only grow and progress through the growth and progress of others.

As a testimony to the spirit of Ubuntu togetherness, we have a custom where every traveler through a country would stop in a village and does not need to ask for food, water, and a place to sleep. As soon as he stops somewhere, people will give him food, entertain him, and offer him a nice place to sleep. This is the South Sudanese version of Ubuntu, which fosters unity, replicated by a society that cares for each other. The true definition of Ubuntu is the iconic leader Nelson Mandela, who with this concept led South Africa to a peaceful transition after apartheid. He never intended to take revenge on his former oppressors. Instead, he acted with compassion and integrity, showing his fellow citizens that to be a better South African, we can act not out of revenge or retribution, but out of peace and love. Often, we see ourselves as individuals who are separated from each other while we are connected and what we do affects the whole country. When you are doing well, it spreads. It is for all humanity and the whole nation of South Sudan.

That is what Ubuntu is all about, it's a reminder that no one is an island - everything you do, for better or for worse, affects your family, friends, society, and the country. It also reminds us that we need to think twice about the choices we want to make and the kind of impact our choices might have on others. Political conflicts, inequalities, poverty, and violence are occurring at a national level, and these atrocities show us that we as a society need to do more to actively live and breathe Ubuntu by putting it into practice daily. We all have a huge role to play, and our actions must inspire others to be part of a better and brighter future. Ubuntu is also about justice for all people regardless of their financial prowess. As much as we need to care for each other, it is also important to practice fairness and equality for all people, regardless of tribe, gender, or social status. Ubuntu is essentially about togetherness and the fight for a greater good and national reconciliation. For this Mandela was prepared to sacrifice his life, and in his own words, he indicated that *'Without Ubuntu within us (South*

Africans), we cannot implement positive changes in our society'. We must help everyone, young and old, to achieve only the best for our common future.

Ubuntu for Reconciliation

National reconciliation plays an important, if not subordinate, role in managing conflicts and post-conflict situations as it carries the hopes and expectations of many people at various levels. The term refers to the restoration of peaceful relations between individuals and communities that were previously in conflict. Reconciliation, however, lacks a universal definition, and more broadly, what is and can be expected from reconciliation varies. As a result, it is easy to broaden the concept and assume that reconciliation will restore interpersonal and inter-communal trust, address historical grievances, and impose moral responsibility on perpetrators without alienating the various communities of a nation. It is highly ambitious, if not unrealistic, to expect a unique effort of reconciliation in achieving all these results. The realization that the process is overwhelming may be obvious, but what are the specific difficulties that the reconciliation process might face? The case of reconciliation in South Sudan highlights some important pitfalls that reconciliation efforts may face.

It is more urgent than ever to invite all peace-loving people to call for a nuanced approach to reconciliation, focusing on the context in which violence has been experienced and on the specific victims traumatized after a conflict. The world's newest state was embroiled in a civil war between the *Government of the Republic of South Sudan* and the *SPLM/A-IO* which began in December 2013 and ended with the formation of the *Revived Transitional Government of National Unity (R-TGoNU)* in February 2020. Specifically, the conflict erupted after political disagreements between President Salva Kiir and former Vice President Riek Machar, who are now peace partners in the interim government. Profound ethnic divisions, sexual and gender violence, and the forced recruitment of child soldiers and civilian deaths are the common tragic features of the civil war that followed the fall of the *SPLM/A* House.

It is not surprising, therefore, that conflict trauma has been experienced at different levels of society. The widespread and seemingly indiscriminate nature of violence has led to a high level of trauma experienced both by individuals and more generally at the community level, particularly after ethnic violence. As a result, South Sudan's already fragile national identity has been further weakened, not least because of its beginnings, as the different communities grow further apart. In a nation with 64 different ethnic identities, such division poses an exhilarating challenge to any reconciliation effort. In this scenario, Daly and Sarkin's work shows that reconciliation is often needed at the three mutually reinforcing levels of society where trauma is felt which is particularly revealing. Focusing on the impact of conflict trauma on the personal, community and national levels helps to shed light on a society's specific reconciliation needs and the inevitable difficulties of implementing them. As highlighted above, violence in South Sudan has led to a high degree of personal trauma, along with a deeply divided sense of national unity. One can assume, first of all, that a broad program of reconciliation can be launched to address these experiences in a go fell swoop. However, efforts at reconciliation in other national contexts show that this is generally not possible.

Promoting a sense of national unity often becomes much easier when there is a background of communion between the different communities, historical or otherwise that can be relied upon in any attempt at national reconciliation. Faced with limited commonalities between communities in post-apartheid South Africa, the *South African Truth and Reconciliation Commission* sought to use a shared history of human rights abuses under apartheid as a common foil for both victims and perpetrators to share their experiences to heal the wounds. Such an approach inevitably leads to the creation of a common *"national history"* which often does not reflect individual experiences of conflict. Indeed, this approach led many participants at the commission's nationwide hearings to feel that *"national history"* did not correspond adequately to their rather unpleasant experience.

While most of the victims of the apartheid regime were committed to reconciliation, the residents of Duduza said that they were not simply prepared to move forward as if nothing had happened. Extrapolated to the South Sudanese context, the Commission's approach certainly arouses sympathy. National unity in a divided society cannot procreate itself without a guiding story that is essentially and centrally managed. South Sudan has fought two separate civil wars *(1955-1972; 1983-2005)* against the North *(now Sudan)* in which the main link that brought together the disgruntled South

Sudanese communities was the desire for independence from the North. After independence was granted in 2011, there was a marked lack of a binding factor on which to build a stabilized national unity. Nevertheless, the introduction of a centralized conciliatory approach to promoting such unity did not provide the necessary space for individuals to reconcile themselves to personal trauma and essentially, to understand their perception of violence. Worse still, such a centralized approach can lead to one community being universally branded as a victim and the other as a perpetrator as was the case in Rwanda's experience. The answer to this problem could then be to take a conciliatory approach led not by the state but by *Civil Society Organizations (CSOs)* like what happened in Northern Ireland. This approach was based on a central fund from which different civil society organizations could draw resources to facilitate different decentralized reconciliation programs.

Although it has led to remarkable personal and community reconciliation that involved giving individuals and groups time to formulate their perceptions of the conflict, there is still a notable lack of national reconciliation. Segregated housing, healthcare, and education are still widespread in Northern Ireland. Besides, the Northern Irish reconciliation experience has benefited greatly from the strong infrastructure, the established civil society organizations, and the available funding in Northern Ireland. However, South Sudan has a much weaker development base. Not only does the South Sudanese government have a nationwide monopoly on violence, but, given the extreme weather conditions, less than thirty percent of the national road network can be used year-round. This hampers the reach of the security services and constitutes a major obstacle to the contact between communities for purposes of reconciliation. Moreover, only 8% of the households are in rural areas *(where 83% of the population does not have a mobile phone, many communities are decentralized, and migrate frequently because of grazing)*, so any decentralized reconciliation efforts could serve to further divide the already divided communities, and are unlikely to make a meaningful contribution to national reconciliation.

This transient view of reconciliation in the South Sudanese context may well point to a host of potentially inevitable problems. But it also shows that reconciliation is not a silver bullet for post-conflict societies. This should not discourage efforts at reconciliation. On the contrary, the analysis of reconciliation at the different levels of society underscores the need for nuanced reconciliation efforts, particularly in the South Sudanese context. It is often impossible to grasp the complexity of traumatic experiences, but in a post-conflict scenario, mediating between conflict-ridden communities can easily evoke a template-based approach founded on successes by similar contexts in other areas within the country. On the contrary, open and sober consideration of the specific difficulties and opportunities that present themselves can serve any reconciliation effort for the better. At the heart of these two grim scenarios is an unpleasant compromise: the need for granting immunity to those responsible for the misery to achieve a permanent ceasefire. In conflict situations, the choice is often made; either peace or justice. But even if the weapons remain silent, how can a process of testimony, reparation, restitution, peace-making, and reconciliation take place when it is those in power who are dividing the society?

In the emerging sector of peace and reconciliation, it is widely accepted that nations will struggle to recover from civil war unless they go through several phases after a cease-fire. This includes finding a common understanding of their recent history to explain what happened; enabling people to tell their stories without fear; and establishing a form of justice that has the credibility of the grassroots to win popular public support. Healing can also depend on recognizing that terrible injustice has been meted out onto the individuals or groups, and thus requires some form of symbolic remembrance through physical monuments or national commemorations. Ideally, a national dialogue can lead to a shared determination for punishing those responsible while preventing similar events in the future. But how is all this possible when the ruling elites in both Syria and South Sudan, to put it bluntly, have no interest in seeing the truth come to light, and hence do not care to end the reckless violence?

It is paramount that mechanisms for a smooth and peaceful transfer of power are given sufficient space to develop. Many South Sudanese communities are still rooted in their collective guilt belief, so the idea of indicting their leaders *(so culpable)* will play into the hands of extremists, rather than breaking the cycle of violence. It is not, therefore, the most effective way to achieve lasting peace, but it must be so for us to have the courage to point out leaders who have committed atrocities and those who have kept the country under the guise of violence and war for many years. The African Union agrees, though it has an uninspiring record in such circumstances and tends to prioritize the legal immunity of African leaders over the needs of the population. So how does a broken society heal when most of them show symptoms of post-traumatic stress disorder? The most common traumatic event is the murder of a close family member, followed by the destruction of their homes. To move forward, restorative justice must rebuild social relationships, including public apologies, the prohibition of public office, and confession. Besides, the guilty political elites, military generals, and leaders must be brought to justice, and those who deserve persecution can have their opinions taken into account by the competent courts of law.

A joint report by the *South Sudan Law Society* and the *UNDP* published in 2015, called for the establishment of truth-finding mechanisms to investigate the decades of maladministration that underlie the current hostilities, rather than focusing on only the events surrounding the 2013 civil war. This process must high-handedly deal with the culture of impunity within the political and military classes, the silence and denial that accompanies massive human rights violations, and the psychological consequences of decades of trauma. Furthermore, the report calls for the recognition that the traumatized population may require a different process of truth-finding and inclusive reconciliation, with the implementation of the one-size-fits-all ideology. Civil society groups in South Sudan have repeatedly demanded that the country's leaders put the interests of the country's ten million citizens above their own. Diaspora groups and local NGOs have pushed for community-based reconciliation efforts, but these critical members of the civil society are often excluded from national or international peace processes.

In a new country like South Sudan with low literacy levels and low participation of the population in the political process, organized civil societies present opportunities for the otherwise excluded voices such as women, young people, and those not in the military, rebels, and militias to contribute to peacebuilding. Grassroots involvement can allow the local ownership of the peacemaking and peacebuilding processes. It could take the form of local truth and reconciliation commissions where people strive to find common grounds for understanding the unresolved grievances that may stretch for decades back. These traditional forms of dialogue may be more appropriate for redress and apology than a top-down mechanism imposed by the national government or worse, by the international community.

A traditional form of dispute resolution called Gacaca was used with some success in Rwanda after the genocide, allowing over a million cases to be heard and their fate determined. This would not have been possible with the conventional judicial structures in Rwanda due to the huge case backlog and the lack of qualified judges that are in touch with the real situation at hand. International donors can also play a significant role in financing local justice mechanisms that have been accepted as credible by the citizens of South Sudan. If that sounds expensive, then consider the cost of an ongoing war in which nearly five million people are starving and dependent on international food aid. Instead of continuing to pump money into the kleptomaniac elite's bank accounts, other donor agencies could support local civil society efforts to offer culturally appropriate processes of trauma counseling, truth-telling, and restorative justice. Anything else shifts the inevitable slide back to a conflict in which the only losers are South Sudan's innocent but suffering citizens.

Think Globally, Act Locally

Applying global solutions to solve local problems

Think globally, act locally *originally began at the grassroots, and today it is a global concept with great significance. It is not only volunteers who are addressing the problems, but also large corporations, governments, the education system, and local communities play an active role in bringing about the desired changes and transformations that benefit the earth. The phrase* Think globally, act locally *or* Think global, act local *has been applied in various contexts, including planning, environment, education, mathematics, and economics. For many environmental activists, the phrase has changed to* Act globally, Act locally, *owing to the growing concern for the entire planet and with it the need for widespread activism all over the world.

In the context of South Sudan, we need more activists and volunteers to solve the country's national and local issues of insecurity, corruption, economic collapse, and the lack of development. For us to catch up with the rest of the region, governments and schools across the country must develop new and innovative ways of teaching peace and harmony as a basis for sustainable development. Today, globalization is considered an important concept for understanding the world. Certain education systems require students from the age of 5 to be taught subjects on global issues. These students are our future policymakers, and so it is essential to teach them the concept of *Think globally, Act locally* to learn how to localize global concepts and how to engage in a common global appeal that leaves no one behind.

Providing free access to schools for poor children in South Sudan is an important area of local engagement and activism. All levels of education are important stepping stones for development, from the basics of kindergarten to the university's advanced courses. Every student should be taught the overarching goals of attaining the quality of life and economic empowerment. Education can break all the wrong cultural stereotypes including those that promote communal violence. It is also a powerful tool for nurturing future doctors, engineers, and scientists to research and cure common diseases to humankind. As a powerful pillar, it can help impoverished countries rise out of abject poverty. Studies have shown that the more the children attend school, the healthier the country's economy becomes. School attendance should not be a lottery for some people, education is even more important in conflict-ridden countries such as South Sudan, and therefore it can never wait as it must be acquired as quickly as possible.

Gender equity means empowering women and balancing academic opportunities to boost a country's income by an average of 23% per year. This can only work if governments invest in schools, especially in rural areas so that the children of farmers and cattle herders do not have to walk for hours every day to and from school, which also strains their parents' resources. In this way, neither the parents nor their children would feel compelled to choose between farming and schooling which also means that even the poorest communities would be able to produce the academic intellect that will develop their regions. Our country depends so much on foreign aid which does not reflect well on its ability to grow itself. Rather, we should consider using the little financial resources we have to empower the local employment sector and support local businesses so that livelihoods can be improved without resorting to the whims of potentially corrupt and incompetent leaders.

Overseas development aid is welcome, but it should never be infinite because we must first rely on ourselves and our potential to develop as a nation. By investing our resources in free and quality teaching and learning, we are investing in our human capital and empowering our youth to be the generation that will end poverty and usher in a better economy. In agriculture, we want people in this sector to be productive by being able to feed themselves, their families, and their communities; increasing food production would also create better employment and livelihoods in rural areas. South Sudan needs to reach out smartly to its other neighbors. Across Africa and the region, the current trend is mainly towards regional partnerships. South Sudan will be strengthened through its active membership in East Africa's regional organizations to develop lasting trade while establishing lasting political links across the continent.

Above all, South Sudan needs to reach out to its people. It must find strength in diversity and build institutions that represent the entire constellation of its broad geographical and ethnic communities. These foundations of a modern, democratic state must be guaranteed: the freedom of expression, full political rights, including institutions leaving no citizen behind, whether in rural or urban areas. In the 21st century, the international community increasingly recognizes the responsibility of governments towards their citizens, including the protection of political space and democratic rights. Popular uprisings in North Africa and the Middle East have shown what can happen when governments are inattentive to their people's needs. The collective commitment must always continue to build a stable, strong, and ultimately prosperous nation.

Democratic governance reduces the potentiality for corruption as it lowers the possibility of scarce public resources being diverted from their intended purpose. However, building far-reaching effective governance takes time. The focus is therefore on defining and strengthening the basic principles of accountability, transparency, integrity, inclusion, and professionalism applied to the functioning of state systems and administration. To this end, the priority programs address limitations and weaknesses in public administration and the capability of oversight institutions. In future plans, this can be broadened to include the private sector aspects of good governance and encouraging the involvement of civil society therein.

South Sudan has rich natural resources, including a considerable amount of fertile, rain-fed agricultural land, potentially irrigable land, water and forest resources, and mineral resources. Considering these natural resources together with a young but small labor force and the current low level of productivity and investment, it is only the small private, mostly family-based, agricultural and livestock sectors that will have the greatest potential for initial new growth. An integrated series of mutually reinforcing initiatives can be planned and implemented to remove the obstacles and achieve the economic development objectives, initially by focusing on renewed rural development and diversification towards broader private sector development.

Before and after the crisis, South Sudan faced deep political, security, social, and economic uncertainties. What do the South Sudanese people see around them at the moment that is symptomatic of the many challenges, past and present? Violent conflicts, militias, hate speech, cattle rustling, misuse of small arms, land grabbing, fear, cyclical violence, anger, mistrust, and others have undermined the potential for peace. That is why some of the main priorities are national reconciliation, security sector reform, justice, and accountability which are precisely the issues that have come to the surface so violently. Ultimately, setting agreed priorities to resolve more than half a century of conflicts will not be dictated by IGAD or the international community alone because the solutions they advance suit the agendas of the ruling party elites and not the problems faced by the South Sudanese. All that we seek is truth, justice, and prosperity to recover from the decades of civil war, conflicts, and poverty. This can only happen if the citizens can freely voice their concerns and participate in implementing global initiatives that solve local problems.

Rebuilding the state

Over the past seven years, internal political wars have become the norm for most of South Sudan's constituents. The conflict has qualified the country for the title of the *Poorest Developing Country*. We are simply rich in principle, but the reality is belligerent. The 2013 - 2020 period after the fall of the *SPLM/A* was marked by serious armed conflicts. Although the picture is grim, it is imperative that a peace agreement prevails and thrives to meet people's expectations. The formation of the *R-TGoNU* is a milestone worthy of being celebrated. Unfortunately, the empirical regularity must offset these positive developments with which peace agreements fail[9]. To ensure that the benefits of reconstruction are broad, we must minimize the likelihood of conflicts flaring up again, otherwise, grievances will fester much as they did in 2016, when the 2015 peace agreement was bridged by a relapse into conflict.

Accordingly, containing and reducing inequality and not simply reducing absolute poverty, could be central to comprehensive reconstruction. This means the transition from war to peace cannot be considered merely a political process, or that the attention devoted to the economic dimensions of the conflict should lag behind the

---

[9] Walter, 2001

political solution. Simultaneously, economists must not ignore the impact of economic decisions on social conflict: conflicts and potential conflicts delay economic growth, development, and the implementation of poverty reduction strategies. Indeed, civil war and conflicts are among the main causes of development and growth failures in today's developing countries, a point that development aid donors are increasingly emphasizing. As societies descend into war, competing groups form to overcome problems of collective action[10]. Ethnicity, whether based on languages, cultures, or other distinctions, can be a basis for collective action against conflicts in poor countries since most are caused by tribal, cultural, and religious differences.

Moreover, as pointed out by Azam[11], organization or action along ethnic lines is often a product of the state's failure to provide equitable public service and social welfare. Conflicts based on grievances about one group's standards of living relative to another's can take on an increasingly ethnic dimension when leaders mobilize their followers by appealing to their perceived ethnic superiority. The greed versus grievance dichotomy is vital to the debate on the nature of conflict[12]. But for any of these forces to trigger large-scale violence, other factors must be at work, especially the weakening of dispute-resolution mechanisms that some call state failures[13].

We can view today's conflicts in South Sudan as a partial or total collapse of the social contract of the agreed-upon rules for the distribution of resources and obligations within the society, and of the associated mechanisms for resolving differences. Moreover, the social contract has economic and redistributive dimensions, which are embedded in fiscal institutions. The social contract, its collapse, and the central importance of its post-conflict reconstruction should never be disregarded. Conflict and the collapse of the social contract might explain why a peaceful social pact or agreement in the pre-conflict phase might become unworkable. Within nation-states, the tax system ensures a functioning social contract as the distribution of public expenditure and taxes is judged to be reasonable, or at least not so unfair to the extent of compelling agitated groups to opt for the forcible capture of government.

---

[10] Olson, 1965
[11] Azam, 2001
[12] Murshed, 2002
[13] *Marshall, 1999*

Youth Policies

The advancement and development of our youths require the promulgation of legitimate policies that support the participation of young people in democratic life, promote social and civil society engagement, and intends to ensure the involvement of young people in social development. Policymakers should examine policies that harness the creativity, innovation potential, and generic skills of the young people. The lack of mutually-agreed-upon policies for combating the exclusion of young people and the unequal distribution of power and wealth is traditionally one of the root causes of civil conflicts. In this regard, I advocate for nation-wide policies that form an organic link between state-building and meaningful youth participation to address the needs of marginalized and vulnerable groups including women and girls, the elderly, the disabled, and young people *(especially the child soldiers)*. Young people urgently need policies that promote transparency, accountability, and common goals between the various local, national, and international actors involved in youth development and confidence building. This promotes the synergy of actions, integrated planning, and operations to put the South Sudanese youth at the heart of the country's sustainable development for generations to come.

The Way Forward

Let's embrace peace to move on

"**W**hat is the source of all these wars now?" A Kenyan reporter asked South Sudanese *President Salva Kiir Mayardit* during an interview in early August 2016 after renewed fighting erupted in Juba, ending the country's brief return to peace. His response was: *"The source of this war is that I requested the ministers to return what they illegally took, otherwise I will have to search for the banks where they hid the money and then take action against them."* He added: *"Some of these ministers had bought apartments, nice houses, and villas, and they are hiding their loot in Kenya, and they refuse to reveal it."* President Kiir was referring to the secretly hidden homes and wealth of his political opponents.

And in a sense, *President Kiir* is correct. Indeed, many *SPLM/A* members have beautiful homes in different locations outside South Sudan, almost all of them being in neighboring Kenya. But *President Kiir* made no mention of his own house in Lavington, nor did he mention his sprawling estate in Luri built while the rest of the country was facing a severe economic crisis. *President Kiir*'s August 2016 statement made no mention of the fact that the cartel which hijacked the state and plunged it into a catastrophic civil war is largely made up of his political allies, and that he is the kingmaker. The rapid accumulation of wealth by South Sudan's ruling clique was as bold and brazen as it was devastating for the country. These kleptocrats conducted illegal businesses with no care in the world as they are sure that even if their behavior was to be exposed, it wouldn't matter because nothing would be done.

The top officials responsible for South Sudan's mass atrocities have amassed unexplained wealth while the rest of the country continues suffering from the consequences of prolonged wars, including famine and the collapse of public infrastructure. *The Sentry*'s investigation suggests that the officials profiled in its report have benefited from the ongoing war and the atrocities it perpetuates and that there has been no accountability for their actions. The information obtained by *The*

Sentry also suggests that many of the top officials responsible for the mass atrocities and human rights abuses in South Sudan are aware of the wealth that others in President Kiir's inner circle have accumulated.

It is not only politicians and the military who are complicit in the appropriation of South Sudan's wealth but even business tycoons. Top officials could not thrive without the help of international bankers, businessmen, corporations, arms brokers, and lawyers who knowingly or unknowingly facilitated their illicit dealings. Weapons manufacturers and arms brokers are facilitating the violent kleptocrats' access to the lethal weapons they use to commit mass atrocities. Arms dealers are only an important but minor part of the problem. The foreign banks that process the arms transactions also play a big role. These banks have shielded government officials as they siphon off large sums that could benefit some of the world's poorest people.

Violence and mass atrocities continue unabated in South Sudan because the perpetrators face no consequences for their actions, and the international banks, multinational corporations, and foreign governments keep supporting their violent kleptocracy. *The Sentry* proposed a new strategy for combating atrocities, such as using the financial sanctions normally reserved for combating terrorism, organized crime, and nuclear proliferation to hold those responsible for these abuses accountable - individuals who have hitherto acted with sheer impunity because they expect no consequences for their behavior. By targeting the network's ill-gotten wealth that the South Sudanese government is trying hard to seize, the international community can exert influence in favor of peace, human rights, and good governance.

This new approach requires targeted sanctions, selective prosecution, and anti-money laundering laws, regulations, and procedures to deter criminals from disguising illegally acquired funds as legitimate income. There should also be a sustained commitment to fight corruption, enhance accountability, build institutional capacity, protecting civil society and the press, and promote transparency in the South Sudanese administration. Both the promoters and facilitators of corruption and mass atrocities should be priority targets for financial sanctions. Whether knowingly or not, many lawyers, brokers, banks, and foreign companies facilitated the misconduct of government officials as a practical matter. Focusing on the anchor objectives not only allows for demonstrable financial impact but also allows influence to be exerted over time as those who are associated with sanctioned persons through their financial transactions recognize that they too are at risk.

As with most sanction orders, some provisions are allowing the sanctioning of individuals or entities providing financial support or assistance, even if only a few high-value or important transactions by an already designated person or an entity owned or controlled by him or her can be considered such. Thus, once a key target is sanctioned, his or her entire financial support network becomes exposed and hence vulnerable. This was a crucial approach in the global fight against drug trafficking and organized crime. Like many South Sudanese state institutions, international efforts to help South Sudanese citizens have been hijacked and diverted by a clique of officials in power in Juba who serve their own bigoted political and economic interests.

Accordingly, all international engagements in South Sudan must be corruption-sensitive to move forward. This means that all international initiatives in South Sudan, without exception - from development aid, humanitarian aid, and commercial ventures to diplomatic engagement, peacekeeping, and security sector reforms - must make a major effort to prevent these efforts from being hijacked by crooked politicians and soldiers. Simply put, if corruption is so universally recognized as the main catalyst for conflict and suffering in South Sudan, then the objectives of the fight against corruption must be at the forefront of any new political initiative undertaken in the country, from conception to planning, implementation, and evaluation. In the future, foreign donors and international institutions engaged in South Sudan should prioritize developing strong public-sector institutions, promote transparency in all government's dealings, close loopholes exploited by the kleptocrats, while allowing civil society and media to play their critical vigilante role.

Who takes the blame?

Long before the South Sudanese gained independence from what was then Sudan, they were known worldwide for one thing: unity. The country suffering in our own hands today is trying everything to survive. Independence was not even voluntarily given to us by nature. Some people paid for it with the hopes that the sunrise generation would turn the lost blood and souls into a fortune for us to enjoy the harvest of our forefathers who sacrificed all for this country's sake. And what was always expected of them was the only sane thing they did and history will remember them in a positive light. Those painful years back, and I mean, during the liberation struggle, the South Sudanese were few, physically weak, and had little ammunition to fight the North (the ruling class), but they had a strong sense of unity that enabled them to do everything.

The desire to liberate this country was once deeply rooted in the hearts of all South Sudanese as they were ready to lose their lives if that would have ended their country's suffering. The world was acutely aware of the determination of the South Sudanese people and of what the oil-rich nation would be like if the South Sudanese were to succeed in achieving their common goal. It is no wonder that all eyes were on South Sudan when it gained independence. Many foreign investors came to South Sudan and people began to glimpse a better future for a young nation in the world. In five years, the country had skyscrapers, excellent schools, roads, and hospitals.

People started to calculate, and indeed they were right - the country was at full speed and unstoppable. The pace was phenomenal and famine was way off. Every South Sudanese had love written onto their faces. Death, as it is today, was only something for the elderly, especially those who have seen their great-grandchildren. Women and girls were not being raped frequently and cases of gender violence were seldom reported. Street children were there, but not as many as today's stray dogs. There was no tribe or ethnic group, we were all South Sudanese and very proud of a unified identity. When something good happens to a neighbor, we rejoice together, and when it is bad, we mourn together. That was humanity at work and had we remained in this spirit of unity, no doubt South Sudan would have been on a safe path of becoming one of the greatest African nations. It would be a peace food basket for the whole region if the government developed a unified vision of unity and love for the country, which would still be intact. But the path we have chosen robs us of the beautiful life that nature designed and placed in our hands for our good.

The future of this country, which today seems bleak, was clear, and what lay ahead of us in those days was nothing but happiness and joy. However, the choice of the other side of the coin changed abruptly without warning. So that is the story of South Sudan.

The way we envisaged this country a few years ago is a thing of the past and this system has already broken down, and if there is one thing we should learn from all this unnecessary suffering and wasteful death, it is the need to remain united and patriotic. We have missed a splendid opportunity that we will never get back for the rest of our lives. If we care about the children of this country who are also the future guardians of this powerful nation, then now is the time that we recollect the broken pieces and reconstruct our nation before it is too late. This is undoubtedly what will free us from all the confines of chaos in which we find ourselves today.

Life is painful...let's learn and gain

Those who, in my opinion, are hopeless or despondent in life cannot be blamed. They are right to say that life is hard. Some have given up because their trials and resilience in education, business, or relationships have not done them any good. As a result, they may think that they are unable to achieve what they are working for, and so they feel that certain things are not meant for them. Some people put in a lot of efforts in starting a business, others gain momentum in their education, study hard to earn the best grades, while others do their best to offer useful guidance, resources, and their time to win people over, but in the end, their efforts appear to be in vain.

Others have health conditions, but despite trying advanced medications, they have not recovered in the expected time. Such people are easy to deceive when it comes to awakening hope in life. One cannot blame a human being who was born naked and raised by a family in a completely new and challenging environment. His or her complaints are indisputable because they are the realities that are part of this life. Suffering is everywhere, and anyone can become a victim, those who are not strong enough to resist the temptations, failures, pain, and rejection can lose hope and give up in life. But even though one thinks life is not fair or the world has denied one the right to life, there are fellow human beings with experiences and inspiring advice who can give refreshing hope. The world is a class, every human being is a teacher, and every situation is a lesson. This means that wherever you are or whoever you meet, you shouldn't be quick to believe that your expectations will immediately be fulfilled as they will teach you either a good or a bad lesson that you will never easily forget.

Disappointments and failures always happen, but you need to learn a life-changing lesson and do something about how you perceive yourself and the chaotic life you find yourself in, just like this little girl who kept complaining to her father that her life was miserable and didn't know how to make it through. She was tired of fighting and struggling all the time. She added that while one problem seemed to have been solved, another one soon followed. And she thought the world always had more problems in store awaiting her. Her father, who was a chef, took her to the kitchen, and while she was standing there, he filled three pots with water and placed them over a fire.

When the water was boiled, he put potatoes in one pot, eggs in the second pot, and ground coffee beans in the third one. And he sat down in silence to wait with his daughter, who was confused by the experiment. He took the potatoes out of the pot and put them into a bowl. He took out the eggs and put them in a bowl. Then he poured the coffee into a mug. He turned to his daughter and asked, what did you notice my girl? *"I can notice sweet potatoes and eggs, and then a cup of coffee,"* she said. The daughter touched the potatoes and felt that they were soft. She took an egg and broke it, and while removing the shell, she realized that the inside was harder than before; and finally, she took a sip of coffee, which was flagrantly tasting with a sweet rich aroma. Then she conjured a broad grin on her little face.

When the father asked the daughter for her interpretation, she exclaimed: *"I don't know what all this means."* Then he explained that the potatoes, eggs, and coffee beans all faced the same adversity which was the boiling water. Yet each of them reacted differently. The potato went in strong and hard, but after getting boiled in water it became soft and weak. The egg was brittle, the thin outer shell protected its inner fluid until it was placed in the boiling water and the inside became hard. Finally, the coffee beans were unique because they transformed the boiling water into something new, sweet, and aromatic. The father then asked his daughter: *'Which of these three are you?'* She kept silent and shed tears. For you, the reader, how do you react when you are struck down by difficulties? Are you a potato, an egg, or a coffee bean? Morally, things happen around us in life, but the only thing that matters is how you react to it and what you make of it. Remember the proverbial phrase *"If life gives you lemons, make lemonade."* The phrase promotes optimism while encouraging a positive attitude

The Way Forward

towards adversity or misfortune[14]. Lemons suggest sourness or difficulty in life and making lemonade implies turning them into something positive or desirable. Life is about learning, adapting, and turning all the struggles we are experiencing into something positive and promising. It is your right to live as a human being. No matter what or who is complicating your life, be sure to learn a lesson and move on. Today, if you are breathing and alive, you still have a lot of chances to make a lasting difference and leave a lasting legacy.

---

[14] "When life gives you lemons". Theidioms.com

Acknowledgments

I am grateful to the Almighty God the grand creator who kept me safe and healthy during the challenging times when the Coronavirus Disease (COVID-19) ravaged humanity as it brought the world to a standstill. I express my immense appreciation to my friends and colleagues whose encouragement and guidance was remarkable throughout the authoring of this book. I would not have completed this piece of work without the unwavering and timely support from the book's editor *Mr. Eric Junior Wagobera*. His constructive counsel and direction broadened my writing skills as I expressed my opinions in a way that made this book's content an informative subject for all the young people across the country to relate with the events described therein. Finally, I express my gratitude to my family whose encouragement and moral support as I wrote this noble book proved to be invaluable. And to my golden parents, I am forever grateful for your tireless support as you always inspired me to achieve more in my life.

List of Abbreviations

AUCPCC	African Union Convention to Prevent and Combat Corruption
CPA	Comprehensive Peace Agreement
DDR	Disarmament, Demobilization, and Reintegration
IGAD	Inter-Governmental Authority on Development
JRS	Jesuit Refugee Service
NEWM	National Early Warning Mechanism
NRA	National Revenue Authority
NYDA	Nile Youth Development Actions
R-ARCSS	Revitalized Agreement on the Resolution of Conflict in South Sudan
R–TGoNU	Revitalized Transitional Government of National Unity
SSBC	South Sudan Broadcasting Corporation
SSPDF	South Sudan Peoples' Defense Forces
SPLM/A	Sudan People Liberation Movement/Army
UNICEF	United Nations Children's Fund
UNMISS	United Nations' Mission in South Sudan
UNPOC	United Nations' Protection of Civilians

www.ingramcontent.com/pod-product-compliance
Lightning Source LLC
Chambersburg PA
CBHW030256010526
44107CB00053B/1742